The Joy
of Sects

Also by Sam Jordison

Crap Towns: The 50 Worst Places to Live in the UK
Crap Towns II: The Nation Decides

The Joy of Sects

An A–Z of Cults, Cranks and Religious Eccentrics

Sam Jordison

ROBSON BOOKS

First published in Great Britain in 2005 by Robson Books, The Chrysalis Building, Bramley Road, London, W10 6SP

An imprint of **Chrysalis** Books Group plc

Copyright © 2005 Sam Jordison
Illustrations copyright © Joe Lobley and Dan Gibbons
Photographs copyright © Sam Jordison except p.79 copyright © Dave Touretzky, p.72 copyright © Digital Vision, p.172 copyright © The British Library, Shelf mark E.618.(8)

The author has made every reasonable effort to contact all copyright holders. Any errors that may have occurred are inadvertent and anyone who for any reason has not been contacted is invited to write to the publishers so that a full acknowledgement may be made in subsequent editions of this work.

British Library Cataloguing in Publication Data
A catalogue record for this title is available from the British Library.

ISBN 1 86105 905 1

Cover designed by Dan Gibbons
Typeset by SX Composing DTP, Rayleigh, Essex
Printed and bound in England by MPG Books Ltd

Acknowledgements

Special thanks to those who have read through sections – or the whole – of this book in various stages of production. The mistakes are all mine, the good bits are all theirs: Barbara, Susan, Elly, Ed, Jon B, John B, 'Bob' J, Mike and Dan G.

Thanks and affection for support, help and general hints and tips:

Elly, Susan, Mum, Dad, Anna, Amy, Dan G, Ed, Jon B, 'Bob' J, Joe, Chas, Tom H, Bronwen, John B, Robin D, Martin, Dan E, Benny, Eloise, Ben G, Rosle, Barney, Tom R, Tim, Rol, Raj, Mike, Fay, Becky, 'Fit' Dave, Luke, Andy, James, Chris, Sorcha, David R, Andrew, Johnny, Naomi W, Alex, Jeremy, Barbara.

Also thanks for invaluable professional advice: Dave Touretzky, Lewis Wolpert, Dominic Streatfeild, the staff at the Bodleian Library, Sean Duggan, David Betteridge, Elder Bauerfield and Elder Roeterink.

And finally, but not least, special thanks to Vanessa for providing such a good place to write it all in.

About the illustrators:

The illuminated letters A-Z were drawn by Monkey And Donkey. The products of unfettered eugenics, Monkey And Donkey combine the mischievous creativity of the chimp with the obstinate work ethic of the mule. They also do buildings, chairs and spoons.

www.monkeyanddonkey.co.uk

The cartoons were drawn by Joe. Born in Romford but raised in Lancaster, Joe likes doodling and avoiding, all the while listening to sad songs.

www.scrib.co.uk

Contents

Introduction

It's great to have lots of sects. The more varied, imaginative and passionate the better. There are few things more stimulating and, in spite of what stern moralists and killjoys may tell you, there are few things more natural.

The human race could hardly survive without sects. Different religions have been around since the beginning of recorded history. They allow us to believe that there's some kind of answer to the chaos, cruelty and crazy physics of the universe. They take away the sting of death with the promise of eternity. They answer all our cravings for power, sex and money.

There may be a great deal of truth in the saying that one person is insane, a few are a cult and thousands are a religion, but it's easy to see why we're all so willing to *believe*, even if the things we believe appear more than a little strange to outsiders. The alternative is to admit that we don't know what on Earth is going on, that there's no reason for us to be spinning around on this cold rock in the middle of an empty universe and that everything humans have ever strived for will eventually be destroyed when the sun explodes.

Not fun at all.

Who wouldn't want to think instead that they're going to be eternally young, perpetually oversexed and permanently happy just as soon as their time on Earth is over? Or who wouldn't want to believe that their beloved dead husband is on his way to collect them and all their friends in a spaceship the size of Texas? Who wouldn't want to hope that they might save the world?

What's more, it's the very strangeness of beliefs that people come up with that make them so fascinating. There are few better demonstrations of the creative imagination and talent of the human race than the infinite variety of religions that it has invented. In the UK alone, it's been estimated that there are currently more than 200 established religions, 500 extreme cults and unknown thousands of more personal belief systems. None of them are dull. Even the Church of England – in spite of its crashingly boring sermons and hopelessly fusty vicars – has provided more than a little interest in recent years with the heated debates about the ordination of women and gay clergy. There are even more American groups and, as you'd expect, most of them are even bigger, brasher and bolder. And as for the Japanese ...

No one book can hope to list all the odd beliefs out there and tell all their amazing stories. I hope at least that this one gives a flavour of the splendour of sects and proves, if nothing else, that people will believe anything.

Sam Jordison, 2005

The Aetherius Society

Founded: 1955.

Country of origin: UK.

Gods and guiding voices: Mars Sector 6, Lord Buddha, Jesus, Aetherius and many more Cosmic Masters.

Membership: Actual membership numbers are not disclosed by the society, although *UFO News UK* recently claimed that there are around 10,000 people on its UK mailing list alone.

Famous associates past and present: Dave Davies, founder member of the Kinks.

Texts: George King: *Realise Your Inner Potential: A Spiritual Handbook For A New Age.*

Basic beliefs: An international UFO organisation dedicated to world peace and enlightenment. They believe that advanced life exists on other planets within our own solar system and beyond. Spiritual energy exists just as much as electricity and can be manipulated in similar ways. Living beings can channel this energy and use it to heal and uplift others. The Earth is a living, breathing being.

If you're ever out wandering in the hills and you come across a bunch of fifty-somethings, arms raised to heaven chanting mantras, talking about Satellite Three and maybe giving blessings to the Planetary Ones, please don't interrupt them. Leave them in peace. They might

Cult Hero
GEORGE KING

George King's full title within the society was: 'Sir George King, OSP, PhD, ThD, DD, Metropolitan Archbishop of the Aetherius Churches, Founder President of the Aetherius Society.' He also boasted other honorary titles, including Prince Grand Master of the Mystical Order of St Peter, HRH Prince George King De Santori, and Knight of Malta. He was an archbishop of the Liberal Catholic Church and Lord of the Manor Of Allington (a title he bought in 1991).

King probably deserved all these titles – at least if we are to believe his own writings about his dramatic and heroic life. In *You are Responsible*, for instance, King describes a visit in an out-of-body state to Mars, where he is wounded by a dwarf with a ray gun. Later, he is commandeered to help the Martians destroy an intelligent meteorite that is attacking their space fleet. King finally defeated the sentient lump of rock 'with a weapon of love'. Thanks George!

be more than just amusing eccentrics; they could well be members of the Aetherius Society working on Operation Prayer Power – and if they're right in their beliefs, they're doing you a big favour.

Operation Prayer Power had its origins on 8 May 1954. On that spring day, George King, a 35-year-old taxi-driver from North London, was interrupted while doing the washing-up by a voice that seemed to come from inside his head. 'Prepare yourself!' it ordered. 'You are about to become the Voice of the Interplanetary Parliament.' Not surprisingly, George dropped the plates he was holding.

This was the first of many intergalactic messages that George King would claim to channel during his lifetime. After finishing the washing-up he began to receive communications from a 3,546-year-old Venusian who went under the pseudonym of Master Aetherius. Next, he received messages from a whole range of intelligent beings. King called them The Cosmic Masters. Among their number were the Lord Buddha, Jesus (who, it turns out, also came from Venus), Count Saint-Germain and another extraterrestrial known as Mars Sector 6.

By 1955 King was holding regular public meetings in front of steadily increasing audiences. His inspired teachings offered solace in the contemporary Cold War climate, and gave hope against the threat of imminent nuclear holocaust. At the meetings, King allowed the Cosmic Masters to speak through him, while faithful acolytes transcribed everything he uttered (by the end of his life more than 600 of these transmissions had been recorded). Aetherius in particular was full of useful advice. He described how to make health-giving tonics out of water and fruit juice and advised Earthlings not to sit with their back facing the engine on train journeys. He also divulged a wealth of fascinating information about the geography of the moon, which he said was inhabited by bodiless creatures that lived in plastic bubbles beneath the weightless moon rocks.

The Cosmic Masters weren't just about passing on health tips and lessons in extraterrestrial geography. King claimed that they were vital in protecting the people of Earth. He said they actively prevent ecological disasters, as well as cosmic warfare, and that they man flying saucers which hover constantly around the Earth protecting us from evil and warning about imminent attacks. At one point, the Cosmic Masters even made an invisible barrier around the planet to shield it from destructive forces. Despite these efforts, however, George King feared that Earth was under attack from 'The Black Magicians', who wished to enslave its inhabitants.

An even bigger threat than the Black Magicians was humanity itself. King maintained that our end would actually come about as a result of us acquiring advanced technology and increased materialism without correspondingly improved spiritual awareness. Hope for salvation lay in the healing energy that the Masters were already sending to Earth, but also in a number of missions they asked George King to instigate.

Operation Prayer Power is one such mission. The aim is to store the energy created by chanting and praying on the world's holy mountains so that the resulting 'prayer energy' can be sent out in a highly

concentrated form to areas that most need it. This unique and beneficial energy is controlled by co-operating Cosmic Masters, who redirect it using a mechanism called the Spiritual Energy Radiator.

That's why, at certain key times of year, members of the Aetherius Society can be found carrying out their rites on high ground in the UK and beyond. Even though King passed away in 1997, they're soldiering on, following his teachings while they await a new leader (who, a prophecy says, will be tall and wear 'soft-topped' shoes that contain no animal products). If you do come across them chanting their mantras, don't worry. You should maybe even count yourself lucky. Although the Aetherius Society are often listed in books about cults and secretive religious organisations, there have been few authors who have concluded that they're anything other than a benign presence in the community of UFO-based new religions. A spokesman for the society told me that they certainly wouldn't consider themselves a cult and that they're 'strongly opposed to the negative practices of such groups'. Speaking with refreshing honesty, he also added that there are elements to the Aetherius belief system 'which to some people might seem absurd'.

The Apostles of Infinite Love
Founded: 1951.
Country of origin: Canada.
Gods and guiding voices: 'God'.
Membership: About 400 fully fledged with another 3,000 supporters.

In spite of their fun-sounding name, the Apostles of Infinite Love are actually a hardline ultra-right-wing Catholic splinter group whose members are required to pledge themselves to a life of chastity.

They are descended from an organisation founded by Michael Collin, a former Catholic priest who was excommunicated from the Roman Church in 1951 after declaring himself to be the real Pope, Pope Clement XV. Collin was a fierce fire-and-brimstone preacher, appalled by what he saw as the moral slackness in the official Catholic Church and in its overseer 'the Anti-Pope'.

Collin predicted that 20 February 1969 would be a catastrophic day for the whole world, wiping out most of humanity. When the prophecy failed to come true, he accused his detractors of 'quibbling over dates'. Among Collin's more unlikely supporters at this time were members of a Danish UFO cult called IGAP (International Get Acquainted Program), as well as one Gaston Tremblay, whom Collin named as his successor. Tremblay soon fell out with Collin, but not before he'd established himself on a monastery compound near Quebec in Canada, assumed the title of Pope Gregory XVII and established the name 'The Apostles of Infinite Love'. Since then, the group has been plagued with controversy thanks to their scary doomsday prophecies and frequent accusations of mind-control. More recently, like the Roman Catholic Church, the group has been plagued by accusations of child abuse directed against individual members (including Tremblay/Pope Gregory himself). In contrast to the accusations made against the Catholic Church, however, none of these sex abuse charges has yet been proven in court.

Aum Shinri Kyo
Founded: 1987.
Country of origin: Japan.
Gods and guiding voices: Shoko Asahara.
Peak membership: 40,000.
Current membership: 1,500 (under the new name of Aleph).
Basic beliefs: Outsiders are bad. They should probably die.

There are so many bizarre cults and extreme religious groups in Japan (183,000 according to one count) that neither the police nor the press paid much attention to Aum Shinri Kyo – until it was too late.

The group smashed their way into the world's consciousness when they released deadly sarin nerve gas into a Tokyo subway tunnel in 1995. Launched during rush hour, the attack killed twelve people and left 5,500 in need of medical attention.

Police investigators and the world's press were then astounded to discover that this well-organised sect had huge stockpiles of gas, weapons and hallucinogenic drugs and that nearly 40,000 people (many in Russia and South Korea as well as Japan) had pledged unswerving allegiance to its leader, Shoko Asahara.

Asahara, a professed admirer of Hitler, was a chubby, nearly blind yoga teacher, who claimed he could levitate, predicted nuclear Armageddon and nearly always wore pyjamas. Before the events in 1995, when he was eventually found cowering Saddam-style in a hole hidden within his compound at the foot of Mount Fuji, his only run-in with the police had come in the 1980s when he was fined for selling a concoction brewed from orange peels that he claimed was a traditional Chinese herbal cure named 'Almighty Medicine'.

Since that low point, Asahara rapidly gained wealth and power. When they searched his office in 1995, police discovered 22lb of gold and the equivalent of £5million in hard cash. He used to drive around in a white Rolls-Royce and was served by followers catering to his every need – and obeying his every command. There was a strict hierarchy of thirteen levels, with specially coloured uniforms denoting which class each belonged to. The privileged were allowed to drink Asahara's bathwater to aid enlightenment. For those at the bottom, life was tough. Children seem to have suffered the most. It's claimed that they were only allowed to wash once a week, had little to eat and were often thrown into solitary confinement. Some even had their eyebrows dyed green and many were compelled to wear special battery-powered headgear designed to produce the same electronic frequency as Asahara's own brainwaves.

In spite of all the extreme behaviour, the reasons for the sarin attack are shrouded in mystery. Some say Asahara was preparing for a war on the Japanese state or that the gassing was carried out to pre-empt a police raid on his compound, but these are little more than theories. Asahara himself, now under sentence of death from the Japanese court, has said nothing that makes sense to outsiders.

Alarmingly, his followers are once again increasing in number, under the new name of Aleph. Their desire to fulfil his bizarre teachings to the letter is proving lethal. Dozens are thought to have died, especially during dangerous purification rites involving bathing in scalding water, and rituals using samurai swords to beat out bad karma. By 2005 the cult, which had shrunk to a mere handful of people after the sarin attack in 1995, had more than 1,500 members. The body count is still rising.

Bhagwan Shree Rajneesh and the Sannyasins AKA Osho

Founded: 1971.

Country of origin: India.

Gods and guiding voices: The Hindu pantheon, Bhagwan Shree Rajneesh.

Peak membership: 30,000 plus.

Current membership (under the new name of Osho): Figures not available.

Basic beliefs: An amalgam of Western psychotherapeutic practices and Eastern religion. Bliss is a birthright. God is the universal consciousness and the enlightened Bhagwan himself is the beginning of a totally new religious consciousness. Man determines what conduct is permissible.

Bhagwan Shree Rajneesh had a simple commandment for his followers, the Sannyasins: 'Enjoy!' Unlike other more ascetic gurus to have emerged from India in the 1960s and 1970s, he demanded little from his followers in the way of renunciation – and lots in the way of carnal pleasure. 'Wait not for Godot!' he preached. 'The more you risk, the more you grow.' His was an intoxicating promise: enlightenment, bliss and lots and lots of sex.

The ashram he established in Poona in India in 1974 quickly became a New Age Mecca. It attracted thousands of young Western disciples sold on the charismatic teacher's mercurial wit and unique brand of Eastern mysticism. Marked out by their happy expressions and orange clothes (dyed at the Bhagwan's instigation, to reflect the colour of the sun) they quickly spread their guru's teachings and popularised his unique forms of taboo-breaking therapies. In these sessions, known as dynamic meditation, pupils were encouraged to destroy their religious and social conditioning to find out who they really were. They wore blindfolds – or nothing at all – and explored their deepest selves by screaming, fighting and, inevitably, shagging. Broken limbs were common, as were broken relationships. The latter came thanks to the teachers' propensity to encourage their students to watch their partners having sex with another person – so they could confront the emotions that this betrayal provoked.

In spite of, or maybe even because of, these extreme practices, the 'Rajneeshees' continued to expand in number. Soon they spread out across Europe, establishing themselves in stately homes like the one they named 'Medina Rajneesh' in Suffolk, where 400 of the Bhagwan's followers established themselves in the early 1980s – seemingly in utopian contentment.

Sadly, there were a few signs that all was not well in paradise. One of Bhagwan Shree Rajneesh's more chilling suggestions was that prominent female followers should become sterilised so that they could better practise his teachings. Ugly rumours of child abuse and the destruction of family life slowly began to surface. The guru's ever increasing wealth also began to attract the unwanted attention of the Indian tax authorities.

To escape from a whopping bill, Rajneesh packed up his 150,000-volume library and, claiming medical problems, entered the United States (along with twelve tons of luggage). It was there that things really fell apart. Shortly after he'd settled his followers in a 60,000-acre $6 million ranch on semi-desert scrubland near the small town of Antelope in Oregon, Bhagwan Rajneesh took a vow of silence (or as, he put it, he determined on a course of 'speaking through silence'.) The day-to-day running of the huge community fell to his follower, Ma Anand Sheela.

Sheela took to wearing robes and calling herself 'queen'. Fences, complete with guard towers, went up around the compound and disciples armed with Uzis patrolled the Bhagwan's residence. Many of the commune's 15,000 members were forced to do twelve hours work a day for no pay. While they succeeded in clearing and planting 3,000 acres of land, building a 350-million-gallon reservoir,

ITS JUST A BHAGWAN / CHILDREN OF
GOD REUNION. CAKE STALLS NEXT DOOR

WHAT THE..?

a 10-megawatt power substation and a functioning dairy farm, only Sheela and her coterie seemed to live in any comfort. The others had to endure unbearable hardships.

The most bizarre incidents occurred outside the ranch in the local town of Antelope. The huge numbers of Rajneeshees enabled them to force the results of the 1984 local elections and take over Antelope's local council. They decided to rename the hitherto upright Oregon backwater Rajneeshpuram. When attempts were also made to rig local county elections by shipping thousands of homeless people onto the ranch, resistance to the Sannyasins grew stronger. Sheela responded by having her followers dump salmonella into the salad bars of several local restaurants. Antelope therefore gained the dubious distinction of being the site of the first successful bio-terrorism attack in US history.

Eventually, Bhagwan Rajneesh emerged from his silence and attempted to distance himself from his disciples. He said that Sheela

HOLY SMOKE!

RELIGIOUS ECSTASY

Ecstasy was first brought to Europe by the disciples of the Bhagwan. He had adopted the drug as his new spiritual elixir, and his army of orange people evangelically distributed it around the world. Some even set up laboratories to manufacture their own supply.

CULT HERO

THE BHAGWAN

Mohan Chandra Rajneesh was born in 1931. After working as a philosophy teacher for several years he accepted what he saw as God's plan for his life – spiritually transforming humanity. In 1971 he assumed the modest title of Bhagwan Shree Rajneesh, meaning 'The Blessed One Who Has Recognised Himself As God'. He established his first ashram shortly afterwards.

During his life the Bhagwan wrote more than 60 books and recorded upwards of 500 tapes. In addition to embracing the spirit of God, he also embraced the spirit of the 1980s, accumulating millions of pounds and no fewer than 93 Rolls-Royce cars. He said that he'd lived in poverty and lived in richness. 'Believe me,' he continued, 'richness is far better than poverty.' He claimed to be a man of very simple interests. He was 'utterly satisfied' with 'the best of everything'.

Towards the end of his life, addicted to nitrous oxide (laughing gas) and haunted by the accusations of sex abuse, tax evasion and poisonings, the Bhagwan retreated back to his original ashram in Poona. In 1985 he declared that his religion was dead – and that it had, in fact, been invented by his followers. He said he was glad not to have to pretend to be enlightened anymore. Then, in December 1988, he told his followers that his body had become host to none other than Guatama Buddha. However, when the Buddha disapproved of his use of the Jacuzzi, Bhagwan banished him from his body and said that he was now Zorba the Buddha instead.

He died in 1990, instructing his doctor to dress him in his favourite socks and hat beforehand. When his disciples asked what they should do with him after he passed on he replied, 'Stick me under the bed and forget about me.'

had been running the place like a 'fascist concentration camp' and went on the talk show *Good Morning America* to emphasise that those with him were 'fellow travellers' rather than followers. He also called on the FBI to conduct an independent investigation into the ranch. The FBI quickly found an extensive eavesdropping system that was wired throughout the commune residences, public buildings and offices. They also uncovered a secret laboratory where experiments had been run on the manufacture of HIV as well as salmonella.

Sheela confessed to having a rather 'bad habit' of poisoning people and was sent to jail. Bhagwan Shree Rajneesh himself was charged with criminal conspiracy, 34 counts of making false statements to federal officials and two counts of immigration fraud. He paid a $400,000 fine and was given a ten-year sentence – suspended on the understanding that he would leave the United States. He returned to India in disgrace and died not long afterwards.

Many of the communes across Europe dispersed in disillusionment and surrounded by their own scandals. In spite of everything, however, some remain faithful to the Bhagwan's teachings. His spiritual descendents (now calling themselves Osho) have maintained his ashram in India as a major tourist attraction and spiritual retreat. In England, meanwhile, they have a thriving community in a large house in Dorset, Osho Leela. There, they run 'Singles Weekends' offering parties, meditations, 'bundles of fun and … who knows!'

Words of Wisdom

‘ The problem I had (with my health) was my back … I cannot sit on [an ordinary] chair. Similarly I can use only one car. I have used all cars, and the best in the world; but the seat of just one car, the Silver Spur, fits with me perfectly. It is not their costliest car; their costliest is the Corniche, then the Carmargue. The third is the Silver Spur. So I tried a Corniche – it didn't work, my back trouble started. But with the Silver Spur it has settled completely. ’

Bhagwan Shree Rajneesh

THAT BLESSIT BEEN THROUGH AGAIN

Arthur Blessit

Born: 1941.
Country of origin: USA.
Gods and guiding voices: 'God'.
Famous Associates: George W Bush.
Texts: The Bible.
Basic beliefs: An evangelical Christian determined to fulfil a Biblical prophecy and take the cross to *every* land on Earth.

Arthur Blessit is a one-man evangelical religious movement – with a heavy emphasis on *move*. He's been touring the world since 1969, dragging a ten-foot-long cross behind him.

Before he was a walker, Blessit hosted an all-night Christian nightclub in the centre of Hollywood's Sunset Strip, where he urged all the hippies, bikers and hookers to drop a little 'Matthew, Mark, Luke and John' instead of their customary downers and LSD. At the end of the 1960s, however, Jesus proposed a new trip. He told Arthur to take the cross to all countries on Earth. By the year 2000, the intrepid evangelist had walked through 301 nations. He's crossed Africa, Europe, America and Asia. He has climbed Mount Fuji in Japan (12,388ft) and the Bronzal Pass between Pakistan and Afghanistan (18,200ft). He's walked to the Dead Sea, into Red Square and along the Great Wall of China. He made no exception for even the tiniest nations; even the Vatican City and Sovereign Knights of Malta have played host to the indefatigable fundamentalist. Not too long ago, he surprised the inhabitants of the Orkney Islands with a visit.

In total, Arthur Blessit claims to have walked over 36,500 miles. He says that his shoes last him approximately 500 miles, so it's safe to assume that he's worn out around 71 pairs since 1969. Some of the other statistics he's notched up are equally impressive. He's been arrested for walking 24 times (once near his home in Hollywood). He's also walked through no fewer than 49 nations at war … wars throw up a few philosophical problems for Blessit. It's especially tricky when countries change their names and borders after he's already walked through them. Did God want him to retrace his steps through Kosovo, Serbia and Croatia now that they are no longer Yugoslavia?

Arthur Blessit is currently planning to launch a two-inch fragment from his cross into space. He says that this is so the cross will be lifted up over Afghanistan, Jerusalem, America, Saudi Arabia and the 'earthly domain' of Satan. He has also printed over twenty million stickers bearing the legend 'Smile, God Loves You'. He intends to launch these into space too.

And yes, Blessit is his original name.

Words of Wisdom

❝ God made me for the road! ❞

Arthur Blessit

The Branch Davidians

Founded: 1935.
Country of origin: USA.
Gods and guiding voices: 'God'.
Peak membership: Just under a hundred.
Current membership: Approximately ten.
Texts: The Bible.
Basic beliefs: David Koresh is the David referred to in biblical prophecy. He knows what he's talking about. Damn it.

The small town of Waco in Texas became famous in 1993 as the site of one of the longest and bloodiest sieges in US history. It was then that members of the Branch Davidian religious cult took on the might of the US government – and lost – with tragic results.

The Branch Davidians were a sect who split from the Seventh Day Adventists (see also **Millerites**) in the 1930s. Like their larger parent group, the Davidians believed in an imminent Second Coming. Unlike them, they had been prepared to name a year – 1959. They were sued by their disaffected former members when the year passed without any apocalyptic incident, but survived under the leadership of George Roden. Roden kept his small group of followers together on a dilapidated patch of land near Waco In Texas until 1986, when he was ousted from the leadership by a charismatic former rock guitarist, David Koresh – who was then called Vernon Howell.

The twisted, macabre events surrounding Roden's expulsion from the leadership were a precursor of things to come. Howell challenged Roden to make a demonstration of his powers, persuading him to exhume the body of a former Davidian to see if he could bring it back to life. When Roden agreed to the attempt, Howell and his associates hurried down to the local police station to inform them of this corpse abuse. The police needed evidence, so Howell and seven other men returned to the compound, supposedly to take photographs, but dressed in combat fatigues and carrying assault rifles. A gun battle followed. Soon afterwards Howell was arrested for attempted murder. He escaped the charges, however, mainly because Roden was deemed far too crazy to testify. When asked to describe his occupation he informed the court that he was a minister. And a farmer. And a presidential candidate. When asked if he was the Messiah he replied simply: 'Thou saith it.'

From that time Howell took absolute control of the Branch Davidians. He renamed himself David Koresh, saying that he was the David mentioned in Old Testament prophecy (and just as quickly became known, unavoidably, as the Wacko from Waco). He began recruiting more members (he was particularly successful in the UK – more than thirty of the ninety involved in the siege were British nationals) and transformed the rundown compound he had inherited from Roden into a huge fortified complex complete with swimming pool and underground storm shelters. He declared himself to be a 'sinful Messiah', forbidding his members to have sex but taking numerous 'wives' for himself. One of these 'wives' was just fourteen years old. Koresh also instructed parents to beat their children if they were 'bad', encouraging them to buy a wooden paddle he called 'mother's little helper'. Each child had a paddle with their name on it. Several were beaten until they bled.

It was these disturbing rumours of child abuse, together with reports of Koresh's suicidal megalomania, emanating from a few disaffected ex-followers that began to concern the authorities. When they discovered that the Davidians also had a huge stockpile of arms, including submachine guns, they decided to act. Some say that Koresh had bought all the weapons as a matter of routine: most of the cult's income came from his work as a registered arms dealer. Others maintain that he was preparing for the forthcoming war against Satan. Either way, when the Alcohol, Tobacco and Firearms Bureau raided the Waco compound on 28 February 1993, Koresh and his followers were armed to the teeth.

Subsequent analysts have claimed this raid need never have happened. All the local district attorney Vic Feazell had done when he wanted to arrest Koresh after the 1986 gunfight was to call him on the phone and then turn up at the door with some handcuffs. Koresh, he said, had given him no trouble. He'd even been polite. Other locals pointed out that it would have been far easier to arrest Koresh on one of his regular shopping trips into Waco town centre.

Nevertheless, the raid took place – and it was a disaster from the start. Even If the Davidians hadn't been warned that something funny was going on by the large numbers of TV cameramen lining the road to their compound, they must have had their suspicions when two chicken trucks sped up their drive and disgorged dozens of armed federal agents. By the time they got to the door, the Davidians were ready and waiting. Even so, Koresh decided to open it. It was only when the agents ordered him to surrender that all hell broke loose.

The ensuing gunfight lasted 45 minutes. Four ATF agents were killed, together with one Davidian. Koresh himself was wounded and retreated into the compound from where he began his unique brand of negotiation. Initially, he demanded to be allowed to preach on national TV before he surrendered. When this wish was eventually granted, Koresh said God had told him to change his mind. Now he wasn't going to give up until he'd written the text that would unlock the Seven Seals and bring on the apocalypse. He'd written three chapters when the government forces finally lost patience. It was the 51st day of the siege. Nothing the police had tried so far had worked – and they'd tried pretty much everything. They'd even attempted to flush out the Branch Davidians by blaring an ear-splitting and nerve-shredding mishmash of recorded sounds into the compound. These included chanting Tibetan monks, the sound of rabbits being slaughtered, howling jet-plane engines and, oddest of all, the Nancy Sinatra hit 'These Boots Were Made For Walking'.

Most observers have come to accept the evidence, gathered from FBI recordings from bugs inside the compound, that in the final hours of the siege – after tanks were used to knock down the compound walls and deliver tear gas into the building – Koresh ordered his followers to set the fires that would consume them. Eighty Branch Davidians were killed. Among the dead were seventeen children, and Koresh himself. Autopsy results showed that twenty victims had been shot dead, apparently by fellow members.

In spite of the evidence from the bugs and the conclusions of several subsequent reports, however, conspiracy theories about the end of the siege abound. The most convincing claims relate to the fact that the FBI used incendiary tear-gas canisters (something they didn't admit until 1999) as well as the standard non-flammable variety. Most of the few surviving Branch Davidians certainly said that it was these canisters they saw starting the fires. They are convinced that their companions died needlessly. Several survivors also continue to believe in the power of their old leader. Even now, they remain in Waco, waiting for the earthquake that they say will come shortly before Koresh rises from the dead and The End really does begin ...

Breatharianism

Founded: 1993.
Country of origin: Australia.
Gods and guiding voices: 'God', St Germain.
Membership: 5,000 claimed worldwide.
Basic beliefs: Breatharians believe that it is possible to live on 'light' alone. They say that unpolluted air contains all the nutrients necessary to sustain life and that not eating food will actually increase a person's longevity.

This spiritual diet's most well-known advocate is Ellen Greve, who took up Breatharianism after she was 'told' to change her life by her spiritual mentor, a Frenchman last seen living in the sixth century AD, St Germain. She also changed her name to the more mystical Jamusheen. In 1999 she claimed that she'd spent the last six years living on nothing more than herbal tea and the odd chocolate biscuit. However, when the Australian TV programme *60minutes* challenged her to practise what she preached in front of TV cameras, she quickly became ill. Within 48 hours she was showing signs of serious dehydration. After four days she had lost a stone and although she maintained that she felt 'really good', the experiment was cancelled for health reasons.

Breatharianism received yet more bad publicity when another prominent advocate was filmed leaving a baker's shop tucking into a chicken pie, and again when a journalist sitting next to Jamusheen on a plane claimed he heard her ordering a vegetarian meal before she realised who he was and refusing to eat it.

Less amusingly, but perhaps not surprisingly, the Breatharian diet has also been blamed for several deaths.

British Israelism

Founded: 1787.
Country of origin: UK.
Gods and guiding voices: 'God'.
Membership: Figures not available.
Famous associates past and present: Princess Alice of Athlone and The Rt Hon. WF Massey, former prime minister of New Zealand.
Texts: The Bible; John Wilson: *Our Isrealitish Origin.*
Basic beliefs: Anglo-Saxons are the direct descendants of the ten lost tribes of Israel and the British monarchy sit on the throne of David.

When sailor Richard Brothers discovered that his wife had been living with another man while he was at sea, his reaction was nothing if not original. Rather than turning to alcohol, self-pity or singles' bars, this devastated resident of Newfoundland shipped across to London where he began to call himself 'Prince Of The Hebrews And Nephew Of The Almighty'. In 1794 he published a book predicting that the millennium would begin the following year and that he would personally lead the descendents of the Ten Lost Tribes Of Israel – the Anglo-Saxons and the Celts – back to Jerusalem. He then declared that as the descendant of King David he was the rightful heir to the British throne.

The current incumbent, King George III, was naturally not amused and Brothers was thrown into a lunatic asylum. Not before his book had become a bestseller, however.

The torch was taken up again in 1840 when John Wilson published *Our Isrealitish Origin*, and thanks to the zeal of one of his readers,

Joseph Hine, it reached every corner of the Anglo-Saxon world. Hine dedicated his life to spreading the British Israelism doctrine – now with the crucial difference that the British monarchy were named as the rightful heirs of King David rather than poor old Brothers.

Hine and the various cells of supporters he established around the British Empire have demonstrated a rare skill at finding evidence to support their cause. Naturally, the Bible is a major source of information. Genesis 49:24, for instance, reads: 'from that time he [Joseph] kept the stone of Israel'. Hine and his followers maintain that this must be a reference to the Stone of Scone – the stone on which monarchs were crowned. However, Biblical exegesis is only the start of the story. With similarly devastating logic, they've explained that the word 'Saxon' is derived from 'Saac's sons', which in turn was derived from 'Isaac's sons'. British, in the meantime, comes from 'Berith-ish' because in Hebrew 'Berith' means 'covenant'. Surprisingly, these derivations can't be found in conventional dictionaries. Nor can their theory that 'Union Jack' is an abbreviation for 'union of Jacob'.

In spite of a distinctly unsavoury vein of anti-Semitism that runs through some British Israelism groups, most managed to steer clear of public controversy for almost a hundred years. Then in 1992, an American-based Anglo-Israelite, Randy Weaver, was caught in a police shoot-out over firearms violations. Weaver had become convinced he was fighting off evil robot agents sent by the 'Zionist Occupational Government' (ZOG). He fought it out for over a week until his wife, his son and a US marshal had all been killed.

In contrast, the separate organisation back at the spiritual heart of the movement in the United Kingdom tends to come across as little worse than a collection of unusually patriotic, ageing eccentrics. Rather than killing sprees, their regular newsletter recounts jamborees, bring-and-buy sales and afternoon teas (with scones, cakes and lashings of strawberry jam). There are homely encomiums on the benefits of old-fashioned education and fulsome, adoring letters of allegiance to the Queen. Only deep probing reveals the steely sentiments contained within its pages about discrimination being an 'essential' characteristic of mankind and the strong warnings about God's intention to 'cleanse' his property in Israel ...

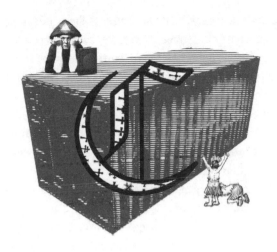

Cargo Cults

Founded: Mid- to late-nineteenth century.
Country of origin: New Guinea and the Melanesian islands.
Gods and guiding voices: The ancestors, some snakes and John Frum.
Membership: Figures not available.
Basic beliefs: The correct practices will bring a bounty of 'cargo' to the believers' island homes.

The famous Cargo Cults of Melanesia and New Guinea provide a fascinating model of exactly what happens when men use religion to explain forces they don't understand – and how easy it is for religions to adapt when their promises are unfulfilled.

The remote Pacific islanders had a long-held belief that the spirits of their ancestors would one day return to them, loaded down with booty. Back in the nineteenth century, they lived in a society where the technology hadn't progressed much beyond the Stone Age. So, when the first Europeans arrived on their shores on huge steam ships bearing gifts that they couldn't even imagine being made, the islanders were pretty impressed. So impressed, in fact, that a new religion was born out of those old beliefs: the worship of 'cargo' (cargo is pidgin for goods of any kind). It seemed that the ancient prophecy was coming true – and how!

Over the following years belief in the power of cargo grew stronger. A number of prophets sprang up claiming divine snakes had given them special knowledge of cargo. They set up practices like doctors, curing afflictions on the basis of their familiarity with these snake-spirits. To encourage more cargo to arrive, they also began to affect the lifestyles of the Europeans, who had now settled on the islands and received frequent shipments of the goods. These quasi-European prophets forced other islanders to do their gardening for them, wearing trousers and hats and copying what they knew of the white man's lifestyle – including sipping at late-afternoon cocktails.

In spite of all these efforts, the prophets still didn't manage to get their hands on much cargo. However, the cult developed further when missionaries started interfering with the islanders in the early twentieth century. A unique form of Christianity emerged. Somehow, the interesting belief came about that Christians worship a god called

Anus. The stories in the Bible, as the islanders saw them, told how Anus created Adam and Eve and gave his treasured handiwork cargo of steel tools, canned meat, matches and rice in bags. However, when Adam and Eve annoyed Anus by discovering sex, he sent a great flood to destroy mankind. Luckily, when he sent the flood, Anus had also given a wooden steamboat to a man called Noah and made him its captain. Humanity survived, but when Noah's son Ham disobeyed his father, his cargo was taken away from him. The bereft Ham was sent to New Guinea, where his descendants were now convinced that they could get his lost cargo back if they worked hard enough at pleasing Anus by singing hymns and praying to him. So, many of the natives did as the missionaries requested. They laboured in their houses, sang their songs and muttered their prayers. By the 1930s, however, they'd worked out that they were being deceived. While the islanders put all the effort in, the foreigners who did nothing received – and kept – all the cargo.

Just as disillusionment began to set in, the Second World War arrived and the islanders once again revised their opinions. Vast amounts of war material were dropped on the islands during the Pacific campaigns against the Japanese Empire. Those who acted as guides and hosts to the visiting American soldiers reaped the benefits. Suddenly, the long-promised cargo was arriving in huge quantities.

Sadly, when the war came to a close, the cargo stopped coming just as quickly as it had arrived. It was then that Cargo Cult activity reached its peak. It was also then that its fame spread around the world as returning servicemen recounted the incredible things they had seen. To outsiders, these stories seemed almost too incredible to be true. In an attempt to convince the cargo to return, the islanders created straw aeroplanes and runways in the jungle (complete with landing lights made from torches) in the hope that they would cause boxes of cargo to fall from the sky again. They carved headphones from wood, and wore them while sitting in home-made control towers. They waved the landing signals while standing on the runways, marched around parade grounds in the jungle carrying bamboo rifles, and stood saluting in front of flags of their own devising.

Inevitably, when the elaborate devices of the islanders failed to bring in the promised loot, disillusionment once again set in. Most of the Cargo Cults have gradually died out. However, on the island of Tanu, more than fifty years since the Americans were there, thousands still hold the belief that one day a GI called John Frum will come down from their local volcano and deliver the cargo of prosperity to each and every one of them. It hasn't happened yet, but the prophecy is open-ended enough to ensure that this time, it will never be proved wrong. Maybe one day we'll all be worshipping John Frum. After all, stranger things have happened.

Chen Tao, AKA God's Salvation Church, AKA God Saves The Earth Flying Saucer Foundation.
Founded: 1993.
Country of Origin: Taiwan.
Gods and guiding voices: The Christian God (not the Old Testament version, though – too 'cruel').
Peak membership: 200.
Current membership: 30 or less.
Texts: Chen Tao: *God's Descending in Clouds (Flying Saucers) on Earth to Save People*; Chen Tao: *The Practical Evidence and Study of the World of God and Buddha.*
Basic beliefs: A quickly evolving theology based on Taiwanese folklore, Buddhism, Christianity and significant current events (around Christmas 1997 the leader, Ho-Ming Chen, interpreted the letters 007 which appeared in the sky as a message from God – unaware that they were an advert for the most recent James Bond film).

Early on in 1998 the residents of Garland, a peaceful suburb of Dallas, Texas, were surprised to find in their midst a group of about 150 Taiwanese people who all wore white clothes and cowboy hats and rode about the quiet streets on bikes.

It was Chen Tao, a group led by the charismatic Ho-Ming Chen, a former social sciences teacher. They had just bought upwards of thirty properties in hard cash and they claimed that they had a spaceship.

'How did you pick Garland?' asked Betty Nichols, an interested neighbour. She was told that it was because, when they say it, 'it sounds like "God's land"'. Unusual as this and other encounters

proved to be, most of the locals only had praise for the people in Chen Tao. 'They are not loud. They keep up their places nice. We could use more neighbours like them,' another resident told a CNN news team.

The police soon became concerned, however. There were (unproven) rumours of child abduction and kidnapping, and Chen had an alarming habit of prophesying the end of the world and imminent nuclear holocaust. The police attention soon attracted the local media and the group decided they'd better hold a press conference.

At the conference Chen explained that 2,000 years ago he had fathered Jesus and now communicated with God via a very expensive diamond ring, which he wore backwards on his hand. Then Chen introduced the journalists to reincarnations of both Jesus Christ and the Buddha (an eleven-year-old and an eight-year-old, both from

Taiwan). He also showed them round the group's 'Godplane', a spaceship complete with wooden deck, cinder blocks, rubber tyres, pole lanterns, captain's chair and a barbecue where one might expect to find the control panel.

This Godplane, capable of holding 100,000 people, was going to lift the repentant out of trouble when Armageddon came in 1999. The full details of how this would happen were due to be divulged at midnight on 25 March when God was due to broadcast on Channel 18 of the local cable network.

When the appointed time for this miraculous broadcast arrived, however, Chen and his followers were surprised to find that the cable network wasn't running any programmes at all. All that they could see on the screen was snow.

The 'God programme' had been due to run until 31 March, when God would come to Earth and shake hands with everybody in the world and speak to them in their own language. When this didn't appear to have happened either, Chen told another press conference of local reporters: 'Since God's appearance has not been realised, you can take what we have preached as nonsense.'

He then gave them ten minutes to either stone him to death or to crucify him as a false prophet. No one took him up on his offer and Chen walked away unscathed. Soon he had come up with an explanation for God's failure to come down to Earth: God had entered the bodies and souls of all those present and anyone who didn't see him was denying their identity as humans.

Words of Wisdom

‚ If you often eat the buttocks of chicken, you will soon find you have a pain in your ass. **,**

Ho-Ming Chen

Words of Wisdom

❛ We have been to the North Pole, last year. People might, people can gain a better understanding if they can remember the movie *Superman II*. He was also bound to the North Pole, and we were also instructed by God to go to the North Pole. **❜**

Ho-Ming Chen

God's Salvation Church was never the same again, however. Many of the members (whose tourist visas were about to run out anyway) went back to Taiwan. Chen and a few of the most dedicated moved to the small town of Lockport in New York State, where Chen wrote a number of letters to the president and tried to interest pharmaceutical companies in his 'universal vaccine', which he said would cure AIDS among other things. Little has been heard of him since 2003, however, when his website disappeared from the Internet.

Christian Voice

Founded: 1994.

Country of origin: UK.

Gods and guiding voices: 'God'.

Membership: No official figures available other than the statement that they are 'bigger than David's Band, but not as big as Biblical Armies'.

Texts: The Bible; Stephen Green: *Britain In Sin.*

Basic beliefs: Jesus Christ is the Almighty Son of God who will return to Earth In fire and glory. All the same, naughty liberals are bullying him.

A lot of people achieve their five minutes of fame by appearing on the *Jerry Springer Show* and starting fights. Stephen Green, the evangelical founder of Christian Voice, achieved his by starting a fight with a by-product of the *Jerry Springer Show, Jerry Springer: The Opera.*

When the BBC broadcast a performance of the opera in 2005, Christian Voice orchestrated huge protests. The Christians were especially upset at the Jesus character in the opera calling himself 'a bit gay'; which suggests that they're as homophobic as the show itself was sacrilegious. They also calculated that the show contained no fewer than 8,000 expletives (which would add up to more than one 'fuck' every second). This figure puzzled the show's producers until they worked out that it had been reached by multiplying the number of swear words in the script (less than 300) by the number of members of the chorus who sang them.

In all the BBC received more than 47,000 complaints (many from people who later admitted that they hadn't even seen the 'blasphemous' programme). When Christian Voice published the names and addresses of several BBC executives on their website, the men in suits also received several death threats from evangelicals who were determined not to turn the other cheek. Christian Voice's resolve was shown even more powerfully when their strident protests 'persuaded' the cancer charity Maggie's Centres to turn down a large donation from the opera.

This last move was especially ironic given that Christian Voice claims to be a 'pro-life' organisation. This anti-abortion stand fits in with the rest of Green's mission to return Britain to the more Christian 1950s. Since that time, he claims, blasphemy and profanity have flooded into national life. He says he can cite 57 laws that have corrupted Britain since the ascension of his beloved Queen Elizabeth II. *Jerry Springer: The Opera* is a symptom of all this, but Green also has much wider targets. Divorce and homosexuality trouble him – especially the fact that there are (horror of horrors) gay policemen and the police even seem to stick up for homosexual rights; rather than opting for the presumably far more Christian option of persecuting them. More unusual concerns of Green's include the European Union (an 'antichrist', 'totalitarian' regime) and the Hindu religion, which is, apparently, 'a manifestation' of Satan.

The Coalition Against Civilisation

Founded: They say they aren't an organisation, so they were never 'founded'.
Country of origin: USA.
Gods and guiding voices: Nature.
Texts: John Zerzan: *Future Primitive*.
Basic beliefs: Have upped the 'anti' further than any other oppositional group. They're anti-everything. They don't just object to aspects of modern society – they want to annihilate the whole system root and branch.

The Coalition Against Civilisation are careful to emphasise that they are not 'an organisation', since organisations are 'power groups' and power is the basis of civilisation. They are, they say, a loose collection of 'anarcho-primitivists'. Their aim is to return to the condition of the supposedly egalitarian and leisure-rich nomadic groups that mankind lived in before civilisation started getting in the way. To return to this blissful stateless state, humanity needs to destroy every invention since the beginning of agriculture. In fact, agriculture's out the window (or rather, cave entrance) too, since it was settling down and growing stuff and owning land that started all those power structures that oppress and destroy us today.

Confusingly, in spite of their anti-technology beliefs, the coalition have published their manifesto on a rather slick website. And yes, you can buy a T-shirt.

Creflo Dollar Ministries

Founded: 1986.

Country of origin: USA.

Gods and guiding voices: 'God'.

Membership: Dr Dollar's World Changers Church has a congregation of around 24,000.

Texts: The Bible; Dr Dollar: *The Image of Righteousness, Lord Teach Me How to Love*; Dr Dollar: *No More Debt!*.

Basic beliefs: A nondenominational Christian church teaching total life prosperity – spiritual, physical, mental, emotional and (especially) financial wellbeing.

Few preachers have had a more appropriate surname than Dr Creflo Dollar. He knows how to get rich. In fact he claims to be in touch with 'the Biblical formula' on how to increase earnings. It's simple: if you give him a seed, he will sow that seed and you will receive the bountiful harvest.

Dr Dollar and his ministries – Creflo Dollar Ministries and World Changers Ministries – are leading exponents of prosperity theology, the tempting teaching that anyone who gives money to God will receive far more in return. Support us with a monthly pledge, suggests the website, quoting Philippians 4:17: 'Not because I desire a gift: but I desire fruit that may abound to your account.' This generous attitude towards receiving money for the benefit of the donator is replicated in the bucket-sized donation boxes in Dr Dollar's 8,000-seat World Changers Church; in the requests that members of the church give it a tithe; and the frequent appeals for money on the worldwide 'Changing Your World' television and radio broadcasts.

Any sceptics feeling doubtful about the efficacy of prosperity theology need look no further than Dr Dollar himself. He's living proof that it works – for him. He lives in a million-dollar home and drives a Rolls-Royce. 'When I'm pursuing the Lord,' he says, 'those Rolls-Royces are pursuing me.'

HOLY SMOKE!

TRAFFIC COP

In December 1999, 100 Fulton County police officers were admonished by the county's ethics board for accepting $1,000 each from Dr Dollar. Dollar said that he sent the money to recognize the officers' service to the community. However, the gift was criticised because it was given a month after two US-style traffic tickets Dollar had received (for running a red light and failing to have proof of insurance for his Jaguar) were downgraded to warnings.

Words of Wisdom

❝ I rave;
and I rape and
I rip and I rend ❞

Aleister Crowley

A Silly Old Cult!
Aleister Crowley

Alive: 1875–1947.

Country of origin: UK.

Gods and guiding voices: Aiwass, Isis, Satan, the stars, free will.

Famous associates past and present: L Ron Hubbard, W Somerset Maugham, Jimmy Page, WB Yeats.

Texts: (all by Aleister Crowley) *The Book Of Law*; *The Book Of Lies*; *Rites of Eleusis*; *Liber Aleph*; *Book Four*; *Magick in Theory And Practice*; *The Book Of Thoth*; *The Confessions Of Aleister Crowley*; *The Diary Of A Drug Fiend*; *The God Eater*.

Basic beliefs: There is no law beyond doing what you will. You have no right but to do your will. Anal sex helps make magic.

It says something about the character of Aleister Crowley that the nickname 'The Beast 666' was given to him by his own mother. So, too, does the fact that he gave himself his other most common moniker: 'the wickedest man in the world'. Crowley was unruly, overactive in mind and body, existed beyond the pale of conventional society, and knew a thing or too about making his own myth.

He's listed here under his own name rather than the group he belonged to because he was a one-man cult-making machine. The societies he set up, controlled – or at the very least strongly influenced – include the Ordo Templi Orientalis, the A∴ A∴ the Church of Thelema, the Golden Dawn (an older society that Crowley deeply affected) and the Mysteria Mystica Maxima (as the leader of this order Crowley took the rather splendid title of Supreme and Holy King Of

Ireland, Iona and all the Britons within the Sanctuary of Gnosis). Although these groups were very different in their names and stated aims, they bore the unmistakable imprint of Crowley's personality, his dedication to the occult and the religious philosophy he called *Thelema* (a word derived from the Ancient Greek for 'will').

Thelema took a number of years to develop. The young Aleister had been forced to study the Bible thoroughly by his fierce fire-and-brimstone preaching father and found it full of inconsistencies. Like Anton LaVey (founder of the **Church of Satan**) after him, he especially objected to what he saw as all life's enjoyable and worthwhile activities being labelled as sinful. In response, he dedicated his life to creating his own philosophical system. In 1904, while holidaying in Cairo, he claimed to have a mystical experience in which the god 'Aiwass' dictated to him the 'Book of Law'. This was to become the benchmark of *Thelema* and every society Crowley controlled – especially thanks to its famous maxim: 'Do What Thou Wilt Shall Be The Whole Law.'

Typically, many of the ideas in this supposedly supernaturally inspired book were actually borrowed. Rabelais had already come up with the aphorism '*Fay ce que vouldras*' (do what you like) and the Elizabethan alchemist and magician John Dee had already urged, 'Do that which most pleaseth you.' All the same, Crowley made the ideas all his own and developed them into a unique (and still influential) form of occult science. *Thelema*, for Crowley, was magick and inspired magick (Crowley added the 'k' to the word magic, supposedly in

45

universe. And who is this dog? Is it not the name of God spelt Qabalistically backwards?'

Aleister Crowley described Lewis Carroll as 'that most holy, illuminated man of God'. He said that: 'his masterly treatment of the identity of the three reciprocating paths of Daleth, Teth and Pe is one of the most wonderful passages in all Holy Qabalah. His resolution of what we must take to be the bond of slavery into very love, the embroidered neckband of honour bestowed upon us by the king himself, is one of the most sublime passages in this class of literature.'

Peter Pumpkin Eater, Had a wife and couldn't keep her, He put her in a peanut shell; Then he kept her very well.

In a footnote, the wickedest man in the world warned: 'If this is thought to be a joke

reference to the Greek *kteis*, a word for female genitalia). He was determined to live his life practising this occult science – and according to the inclination of his own will.

Luckily enough for Crowley, this meant that he could also indulge his twin passions for kinky sex and strong drugs. The rites he devised generally contained some kind of 'sex magick', including plenty of fairly standard homosexual and heterosexual sex, masturbation, ritual buggery (apparently magickally more potent than vaginal copulation), bacchanalian dancing, whippings, burnings, coprophilia and bestiality. On a particularly good night, he could even be found drinking cat's blood and getting blasted on hallucinogenic drugs while waving huge swords around.

In furtherance to the desire of his will, he visited hundreds of prostitutes and claimed to have slept with women of between eighty and ninety nationalities. As well as the obvious, he said, this broad sexual experience helped to prove one of his fundamental beliefs: every sexual moral principle was upheld somewhere by somebody – and ignored elsewhere – proving that morality was beyond judgemental consideration.

Crowley's drug intake, too, was prodigious. He was a habitual pipe and cigarette smoker and regular drinker, and is also known to have experimented regularly with ether, opium, cocaine, anhalonium (peyote, which he generally mixed with chocolate), Myriam Deroxe pills (a mixture of morphine, opium and sparteine devised by Crowley and named after a lady friend), ethyl alcohol (which he affectionately called Ethel), morphine, hashish, and mushrooms of various sorts. Oh, and heroin. This last drug had a particularly sad effect on Crowley, frequently reducing him to hopeless addiction and thereby undermining one of his central tenets about the power of the mind and will.

Indeed, by the end of his life Crowley was rather a tragic figure, hounded out of many countries and societies because of his reputation and the rituals he practised. At home in England he was a laughing stock. The papers would mercilessly vilify him and he was unable to resort to the libel laws as it was widely considered that he had no reputation to defend. In 1934 he had even had to declare himself bankrupt after losing a case in which the judge said to the jury: 'I thought that I knew of every conceivable form of wickedness. I thought that everything which was vicious and bad had been produced at one time or another before me. I have learned in this case that we can always learn something more if we live long enough. I have never heard such dreadful, horrible, blasphemous and abominable stuff as that which has been produced by the man [Crowley] who describes himself to you as the greatest living poet.'

Crowley died in near poverty. Popular myth has it that his last words were, 'I am perplexed.' Actually, his friend Deirdre McAlpine, who was by his side at the time, claimed that he said, 'Sometimes I hate myself.'

Characteristically, however, Crowley has managed to come through it all to have the last laugh. This process started with his

the reader is one useless kind of fool.' Meanwhile, if the reader believes that Crowley really thinks the maker of the rhymes had any kind of occult intention then, 'he is another kind of fool'.

HOLY SMOKE!

OLD MOTHER ... HUBBARD (PART 2)

The founder of Scientology L Ron Hubbard was for a while one of Crowley's acolytes. Together with Jack Parsons, a pioneering rocket scientist, Hubbard tried to carry out a ritual Crowley called 'Babalon Working'. Crowley wasn't impressed. He wrote: 'Apparently Parsons or Hubbard or somebody is producing a Moonchild. I get frantic when I consider the idiocy of these louts.'

Hubbard later claimed that he had become involved with *Thelema* because he intended to break up the 'evil' black-magic group. However, in 1952 he was recorded on tape recommending that his students read *Magick In Theory And Practice* written by 'the late Aleister Crowley, my very good friend'. Crowley, for his part, had always remained more sceptical of Hubbard. He described the American's relationship with Parsons as 'the ordinary confidence trick', a suspicion that was borne out when Hubbard ran off with Parsons' wife and a considerable amount of his money.

funeral, which the tabloid press was outraged to declare 'a black mass'. Since then his reputation has gone from strength to strength. The societies he helped mould still survive in various forms around the world. His prolific output of books are regarded as occult classics. The man himself has become a countercultural icon. His face appeared on the cover of the Beatles *Sgt Pepper* album. Led Zeppelin's Jimmy Page bought Crowley's old house in Scotland and filled it with related ephemera. Meanwhile, the wicked old man has probably been namechecked in more dodgy heavy-metal tracks than Harley Davidsons, hot chicks and 'getting rocked' combined.

A Silly Old Cult!
The Cynics

Founded: *c.* 400 BC.
Country of origin: Greece.
Gods and guiding voices: Zeus and Co.
Membership: Figures not available.
Basic beliefs: Doubt.

The Cynics came to prominence in late-fifth-century BC Athens thanks to the teachings of one Antisthenes, who said that 'I would rather go mad than enjoy myself'.

Offering a way of life rather than a theoretical philosophy, Cynics proclaimed the supreme importance of individual freedom and self-sufficiency. They preached the natural life and rejected with contempt the customs and conventions of their contemporary society.

The most famous cynic was Diogenes of Sinope, a disciple of Antisthenes. Diogenes became known as 'the dog' because of his unusual lifestyle (the Ancient Greek for dog is κυων – the source of the derivation 'cynic'). He lived in a wine barrel. He used to carry a lantern around Athens during the day 'looking for an honest man' (he never found one). He also endorsed theft ('all things are the property of the wise', he said) and claimed to approve of cannibalism.

Legends about Diogenes' caustic wit abound. One tells of the time he was taken to a grand house and somebody warned him not to spit. He cleared his throat and gobbed right into the man's face since he was, he said, 'unable to find a meaner receptacle'. Another tells of how he humiliated the philosopher Plato when he tried to define man as a 'featherless biped'. Diogenes turned up at the next lecture with a plucked chicken, declaring, 'Here is Plato's man.' After that, '… with broad nails' was added to Plato's definition. Once, some poor sucker is said to have mistaken Diogenes for a conventional beggar and offered to give him alms – on the proviso that Diogenes persuaded him to do so. 'If I could have persuaded you,' said Diogenes, 'I would have told you to hang yourself.'

PSST, ITS HIS FORTIETH

" I WOULD RATHER GO MAD THAN ENJOY MYSELF "

The fearsome reputation of Diogenes even reached Alexander the Great. When the warrior king conquered Athens he is said to have been especially keen to meet the old Cynic. He eventually found him sunbathing. He asked him if there was anything in the world he would like. 'Stand out of my light,' replied Diogenes.

The encounter only increased Alexander's admiration. 'Had I not been Alexander,' he said, 'I would have liked to be Diogenes.' Neatly, according to popular myth, they both died on the same day in 323BC. Alexander was 33 while Diogenes had clung on to the life he disparaged until the age of 90.

A Silly Old Cult!
Dame Eleanor Davies
Alive: 1590–1652.
Country of origin: UK.
Gods and guiding voices: 'God', anagrams.

On the morning of 28 July 1625, the 35-year-old Dame Eleanor Davies was lying in bed at her home in Edgefield Manor when she heard a 'great voice from heaven', which informed her that 'there is Nintene yeares and a halfe to the day of Judgement and you as the meek Virgin'.

She believed that the message came from the prophet Daniel and immediately set to work writing down the new insights she had gained. Her husband threw this first book into the fire. In return she prophesied his 'doom' and started wearing mourning clothes. She told him to expect to die within three years; he did, and Dame Eleanor began to attract a following as an unusually accurate prophetess and 'cunning woman'.

She wrote 28 books and tracts, containing a baffling mixture of religion, politics and prophecy, combined with anagrams, puns and dense literary imagery. In these she correctly predicted the impending assassination of the Duke of Buckingham (the favourite of King Charles I who was stabbed to death in Portsmouth) and accurately forecast that Queen Henriette Maria's first child would die and the second would be healthy.

Her fame reached its peak when she wrote a book called *Reveale O Daniel* (the title is an anagram of her maiden name – as written in seventeenth-century script – Eleanor Avdlie) and predicted doom to Charles I. For predicting the monarch's demise she was put on trial. The judges tried to convince her she was crazy and the prosecution used her own favoured methods to point out that an anagram of Dame Eleanor Davies was 'Never So Mad a Ladie' (well, almost – but then, no one could spell properly in the 17th century). Her book was burned and she was thrown into a lunatic asylum, where for years members of the public were able to pay to see her languishing.

Dame Eleanor had the last laugh. She was released and even taken to meet Cromwell after he executed Charles I in 1649. When she died shortly afterwards she was reckoned one of the most successful and consistently accurate prophets in history – although, it must be said, the Day of Judgement didn't arrive as she had predicted.

Divine Madness
Founded: 1991.
Country of origin: USA.
Membership: Around a hundred.

You don't have to be mad to be an endurance runner, but as the followers of Marc 'Yo' Tizer have shown, it certainly helps. Tizer's philosophy has reaped remarkable rewards on the US ultra-marathon circuit, gaining several important wins in races that can be as long as 200 miles.

Members of Divine Madness work hard and play hard. Reports from the 1990s described tough training regimes, but also all-night dance parties and frequent partner-swapping. Tizer is also said to have claimed that he can detect physical problems (and the correct fit of a running shoe) just by pulling on his follower's arms.

Unfortunately, there are drawbacks. In a civil lawsuit filed in 1996, three disgruntled former members claimed that Tizer controlled them through fasting, sleep deprivation, isolation from friends and family, and the prohibition of monogamy. Meanwhile, Tizer's runners' ability to run through walls of pain has caused several serious injuries, and one runner tragically died from a collapsed lung shortly after running more than 200 miles in just 25 hours.

The Emin, AKA The Template Foundation
Founded: 1970.
Country of origin: UK.
Gods and guiding voices: Raymond Armin, pretty colours.
Membership: 2,000 plus.
Basic beliefs: They have established contact with an unseen world.
Ancient civilisations used to know all about this world, but modern
man has lost touch with it thanks to his blind reliance on science and
rationality. The solution to the sick state of mankind is to follow
Raymond Armin's philosophies and believe in the power of colours.

In April 2004, Member Elin Jones surprised the Welsh National
Assembly by reading out some Emin literature: 'At no time will

homosexuality, lesbianism, transvestism, nymphonic or any other unnatural condition or freak practice ... be permitted.' She went on: 'It is against God and creation to worship any symbol in an upside-down condition, or to perform any ceremony backwards. Any offender will be exorcised and excommunicated. This [excommunication] can cause death by spontaneous combustion, petrification and electrical gangrene.'

Electrical gangrene? Ouch. Ms Jones was quoting from 'The Poem Of The Church Of The Emin Coils', a work written by Raymond Armin, the founder of The Emin. She had been moved to speak after hearing that the eccentric movement, under its new name of The Template Foundation, had been given over £100,000 by her local county council

"JUST PROCESSING THE SMOKE"

HOLY SMOKE!

WANKERS

Armin allowed his followers to masturbate – but only once a week and provided that no mental pictures or associations were part of the act – which had to be entirely mechanical.

to set up a holiday centre. Jones said she was 'baffled' as to how the not-for-profit organisation could bring anything into the local economy. Supporters of the Foundation pointed out that this was a document from the 1970s and 'a mistake', but several other Welsh Assembly members also expressed surprise and dismay when they realised exactly who was going to get all that lovely money.

For eight years Raymond Armin, a former encyclopaedia salesman and bankrupt, spent his Saturday mornings sitting under an oak tree on Hampstead Heath until, in 1971, he discovered the Eminent Way. He shortened this to 'The Emin' (which, handily, is also an Arabic expression meaning 'faithful one') started gathering followers and a philosophical movement was born.

Exactly what his movement is about is notoriously hard for outsiders to understand. Although some estimations put Armin's output at more than seven million written words, there are still few people in the world who know what he was getting at. It is at least clear that he thought the contemporary world was pretty terrible and about to destroy itself. He offered his followers a way out of those horrors by seeking all that is good in human existence. Good things included dancing in gowns, astrology, astral travel, heraldry, tarot and belief in reincarnation. Followers were also encouraged to accept the mystical significance of numbers and to change their name to words like Opal or Hope or Wonderful. Colours, too, had special mystical significance, which you'll latch onto pretty quickly if you see any of The Template Foundation's brightly coloured magazines or websites.

Anti-cult organisations described the groups that sprung up around Armin as secretive and exclusive. Clandestine meetings were held around the world for fee-paying groups that superficially claimed no allegiance to the original Emin, but somehow managed to fund a lifestyle for Armin that was so luxurious his Florida home was valued at $3.5million when he died. Ravel's *Bolero* was often played at meetings where the more devoted were observed to chain smoke, a habit mimicking Armin. For a man in touch with the higher worlds, smoking was no longer a harmful activity. 'I'm just processing the smoke,' he explained.

In spite of the concerns of the cult-watchers and vague rumours of coercion and mind-control, The Emin managed to keep a fairly low profile up until after Armin's death and the problems with the Welsh Assembly. The man himself had only made one brief appearance in public in 1983 when the British MP David Mellor stopped him leasing a church hall in Putney because of his fears about what went on there. Armin launched a positive publicity campaign in the local press to try and improve his damaged image. The readers of the *Wandsworth And Putney Guardian* will probably never see anything like it again. 'I reckon,' he said, 'I'm about the most brilliant man you have ever met. I must be to have all these people with university degrees following me … Obsession is a weak word for it. These people would follow me around the world until I die.'

Armin also admitted to an intrepid local journalist that he had been worried by claims made by a few of his more zealous followers that he could kill by thought power, but was now pretty confident that he couldn't. 'I caught a mole in my garden and put it in a jar,' he said. 'I sat and looked at it and tried to give it a cerebral haemorrhage. But I couldn't. If I can't do that to a mole how can I do that to a human being?'

So, that at least is clear then.

A Silly Old Cult!
Exegesis
Founded: *c.* 1980.
Country of origin: UK.
Gods and guiding voices: The truth.
Peak membership: About 5,000 in the 1980s.
Current membership: None (now defunct).
Famous associates past and present: Carole Caplin (friend and advisor to Cherie Blair); Mike Oldfield (musician) attended one of their therapy sessions.
Basic beliefs: Money: good. Leaving therapy sessions before they're over: bad.

Exegesis ceased to exist in the mid-1980s, shortly after then Conservative Home Office minister David Mellor (him again) described it in parliament as 'puerile, dangerous and profoundly wrong'. However, its influence continued to be felt almost twenty years later – especially when one of its most prominent former members, Carole Caplin, became embroiled in a scandal with Cherie Blair, the wife of the British prime minister.

Exegesis specialised in alternative therapy, designed to 'rebirth' participants by encouraging them to face up to their inner fears. Devotees were encouraged to tell the truth at all times, no matter how painful this could be. This rule proved especially tough in sessions where they were made to expound their innermost fears and desires – and tell fellow devotees exactly what they hated about them.

Organisers called it 'raising the confront'. It was at some of these meetings that Caplin, who had once been a topless model, was said to have been seen guarding the doors.

When Exegesis dissolved amid the customary murky rumours of brainwashing and group sex (and strange stories about the unusual marketing activities of its subsidiary company Programmes, said to have used attractive women to help 'persuade' company executives to bid for its products), Caplin set up her own company and gradually established herself as a 'lifestyle guru'. She met Cherie Blair in a gym in 1992, introducing the wife of the man who would eventually assume ultimate control of Britain's National Health Service to healing crystals, and taking her to meet 86-year-old dowsing healer Jack Templer, who worked on her swollen ankles by swinging a crystal pendulum over the affected area. He fed her strawberry leaves that he had grown within the 'electromagnetic field' of a Neolithic circle he'd built in his back garden.

Caplin's relationship with the Blairs took a severe bump in December 2002, when tabloid newspapers got wind of the fact that her partner at the time, convicted fraudster Peter Foster, helped the Blairs buy a flat at a reduced price in Bristol. Caplin has, however, managed to stay true to her New Age beliefs, writing a book called *Lifesmart*, warning of the dangers of red meat, eggs, nuts, fruit, milk, bread and 'stressful' vegetables like aubergine and potatoes. Reviews were predictably damning.

The Family, AKA Family of Love, AKA The Children of God
Founded: 1967.
Country of origin: USA.
Gods and guiding voices: 'God'.
Peak membership: 50,000 in the late 1970s.
Current membership: 8,000.
Famous associates past and present: The parents of River Phoenix, Jeremy Spencer (former Fleetwood Mac guitarist).
Texts: The Bible; *The Mo Letters* (letters written by David Berg with titles like 'Sex Works!', 'The Art of Oh!' and 'Come On Ma, Burn Your Bra!').
Basic beliefs: Hardline apocalyptic Christianity, mixed with the teachings of the group's founder and prophet David Berg. He used to say that love is the law and almost anything is permissible if it's done

Kvm by ahhh...

in love. Especially adultery, wife swapping, lesbianism, incest and prostitution.

Surprisingly – given what happened in the 1970s and 1980s – the Family (back when they were known as the Children of God) started out with strict rules about chastity. The young Californian hippies whom the forty-something David Berg first recruited into his evangelical group were initially encouraged to renounce all their sixties decadence. It was only when Berg started an affair with his secretary that things really started to swing.

Berg was a self-proclaimed End Time prophet who, like David Koresh of the **Branch Davidians**, claimed that he was the David prophesied in the Old Testament. After his trysts with his secretary he began to endorse a radical form of altruism. He taught that the only law was love and that God looks only at the motivation behind deeds. The logical extension of this was that nothing was wrong or unlawful, as long as it was 'done in love'. Polygamy was the welcome (for Berg at least) result of these ideas. The prophet began to work his way through his young female followers with enthusiasm.

In the early 1970s, as the group grew in number and infamy, Berg's doctrine became more and more radical. He took on the nickname 'Moses', as he believed he had a direct line to God, just like the hero of Exodus. He also encouraged his followers to leave America, warning that it was shortly to be destroyed by the comet Kohoute. The fact that he was now being hounded by accusations of brainwashing and molestation may have had a role in this decision too.

The Children of God dispersed across the globe. Berg communicated with them by sending out regular 'Mo' (short for Moses) letters. It was in one of these that he outlined his most controversial doctrine: Flirty Fishing. Attractive female members of the group were told to 'lure in a fish' using themselves as bait. Men were told to give up their wives as a symbol of their devotion to the cause. He even sent his 'Happy Hookers for Jesus' knocking on doors like Jehovah's Witnesses – but they offered something more than a look at the *Watchtower*.

'The only Bible those boys are likely to read is that gorgeous gal with her bosoms hanging out,' wrote Berg, showing a real salesman's knowledge of how to catch an audience. He encouraged topless bathing, free love, lesbianism and even incest in the increasingly pornographic and wild Mo letters. 'God is a pimp!' he exclaimed, as his Flirty Fishers began offering their bodies for money as well as to bring in converts. The 'sex cult', as it was now known, grew extremely rapidly. Unfortunately, since Berg had also prohibited the use of contraception, many fatherless babies ('Jesus babies') were born and the group was ravaged by venereal disease.

Not surprisingly, the extreme practices of Berg and his followers began to attract negative publicity – especially when ex-members (including one of David Berg's daughters, Deborah) started to come forward with allegations of widespread physical and mental abuse and

Words of Wisdom

❝ Receiving Jesus is like going all the way. ❞

David Berg

paedophilia. Berg reacted by lying low and instructing his followers to tell the public they had disbanded. They began to go under various names, finally settling on the Family of Love in 1979, later shortened to The Family (but presumably not in an act of homage to **Charles Manson**). When Berg died in 1994 (almost exactly one year after the date he'd prophesied for the end of the world), The Family apologised for its past actions and set to work improving its public image. A number of charitable foundations were set up. Some of them probably did good work, although ex-members have frequently suggested that some were little more than recruiting grounds for homeless children.

In spite of these efforts, The Family's troubled past has proved hard to escape. Even though they said they were sorry, and set up stringent new codes of sexual conduct, The Family did little to change its hierarchy. After Berg's death, his former mistress 'Mama Maria' Zerby took control of the organisation and many of the same leaders stayed in place under her. Ex-members still complained of extreme practices, like the encouragement for all members to imagine that they are having sex with Jesus while they masturbate.

One of the most virulent critics of Zerby and the group was the son she had with David Berg, Ricky Rodriguez. Until he left the group in the mid-1990s, Rodriguez was called Davidito. He was hailed as a Messiah and had been feted since his childhood. A tome called *The Davidito Book* was even distributed to members, chronicling his upbringing, and showing the baby Rodriguez watching orgies and having his genitals fondled. Perhaps not surprisingly, Rodriguez claimed that he had been sexually abused. In January 2005 he recorded a video in which he can be seen methodically loading bullets into a Glock pistol and vowing revenge on his own mother. He also showed off a large knife, a drill and a soldering iron. He would use these as torture tools, he said, to extract information from people who knew about his mother's whereabouts.

Rodriguez sent the video to a friend and fellow former member of the Children of God, Sarah Martin. Before she could watch it, however, he was dead. He'd managed to track down his former nurse, Angela Smith. He thought that she knew where he could find his mother – and he claimed she, too, had abused him as a child. He cut her throat. Then he phoned his ex-wife to admit his crime, drove his car into the desert and put a bullet in his own brain.

Once again the Family were headline news around the world – for all the wrong reasons.

Words of Wisdom

'Enjoy yourself and sex and what God has given you to enjoy, without fear or condemnation! ... Power to the People. Sex power – God's power – can be your power! Amen? Be a ex-revolutionist for Jesus! Wow! There we go again. Hallelujah! Are you comin'?'

David Berg

The Findhorn Foundation

Founded: 1962.

Country of origin: UK.

Gods and guiding voices: Any and every, with a special emphasis on vegetables.

Membership: The Foundation attracts 14,000 visitors a year and houses several hundred.

Famous associates past and present: The band The Waterboys liked the Foundation's headquarters so much they decided to record an album there and lead singer Mike Scott now lives at the Foundation. Ruby Wax has been known to make the occasional noisy appearance on site – as has the comedian Phil Kay.

Texts: Eileen Caddy: *God Spoke To Me*; Dorothy Maclean: *To Hear The Angels Sing*; Eileen Caddy: *Opening Doors Within*; Paul Hawken: *The Magic Of Findhorn*; Eileen Caddy: *The Spirit Of Findhorn*; Rita Eide: *The Celestial Voice Of Diana*.

Basic beliefs: Members say they are part of a living laboratory where sacred works and spiritual ideas are put to the test every day. Their ultimate aim is to promote a planetary culture infused with spiritual values.

Out of all the groups included in this book, the Findhorn Foundation is perhaps unique in its refusal to adhere to any one religious dogma. It also has a quantifiably beneficial effect on the fragile local economy and ecology of its home in the wilds of Northeast Scotland (bringing in millions of pounds and thousands of visitors a year and pioneering alternative energy usage).

It feels a bit harsh to include them.

Then again, Eileen Caddy and Dorothy Maclean did set the whole thing up because Eileen was instructed to do so by her 'inner voice' and because Dorothy discovered a rare ability to hold conversations with plants and vegetables. Their printing press has published a book called *The Celestial Voice Of Diana*. And prominent members have been known to hug trees and describe it as a 'sexual' experience.

The founders, Eileen Caddy and her husband Peter, were rootless and former hoteliers who decided to live in the sand dunes near the small, isolated Scottish town of Forres after Eileen started taking briefings from her inner voice. Before that, they had been listening more to extraterrestrials. These aliens had told them to cut down all the trees behind the hotel where they worked to make space for special landing craft and the evacuation of selected humans from the imminent nuclear holocaust. Eileen and Peter had dutifully cut down

HOLY SMOKE!

THE CELESTIAL VOICE OF DIANA

Published within two years of the untimely death of 'The Princess of Hearts' in 1997, *The Celestial Voice Of Diana* was written by Rita Eide, who claimed to have channelled the voice of Diana from beyond the grave. In contrast to its fleshly counterpart, Diana's celestial voice was full of homely wisdom and able to promise a 'recipe' for happy living. She also had some pretty startling revelations: like the facts that she was the mother of the Virgin Mary in a past life and that her death as the Princess of Wales was not brought about by plotters in the Royal Family but was actually the idea of some 'higher entities' on the spiritual plain. Shockingly, the voice also revealed that aliens are on their way to revisit humanity and that they *will* probe us.

the trees – but neglected to get permission from the owners of the hotel. Not surprisingly, they were sacked.

Things started to get better, however, once they established themselves in the sand dunes with Dorothy Maclean, who was also in the habit of taking instructions from God. God spoke to her through the medium of vegetables, with particular reference to how best to grow cabbages. The cabbages grew so big in that unlikely soil that Maclean's fame quickly spread and other curious people began to arrive. Eileen, meanwhile, was now claiming a pretty direct line to the 'god within' and proved to be a prolific writer. Her nonaggressive brand of all-embracing spirituality soon attracted even more followers; particularly those New Age seekers who prefer learning how to live life rather than actually living it.

Since then the settlement, which was initially little more than a couple of caravans, has expanded into a huge ecological housing complex and conference centre, as well as a nondenominational 'spiritual community' with hundreds of members. Most of the houses are smart, low-impact, low-energy dwellings fuelled by wind and solar energy, ingeniously made from recycled materials (such as gigantic barrels from old whisky stills). Pedestrians have priority over cars. Parents feel safe letting their children play and roam free outside. There's a thriving mini-economy based on a printing press, a conference centre, educational courses, therapy courses and an organic-box delivery scheme selling produce from the large communal gardens.

Houses within the community sell for upwards of £275,000: a huge price for that empty part of Scotland. Few of the many courses they run cost less than £1,000 per person – even taking into account the discounts they give for people on benefits. They're a thriving moneymaking operation and their on-site café sells the most delicious (organic) chocolate brownies. They've pioneered a practical and impressive form of sustainable living in their hostile part of the world.

However, although they're relatively benign – the worst they're likely to do to you is hold your hand and hug you a *little too* warmly – the Findhorn people are rather unusual. You can tell just by looking at the books in the on-site book store, where titles include *Gatekeeper? What is Enlightenment?*, *The 21 Lessons Of Merlyn*, *Earth Dance Drumming*, *Baby Om*, *Science and Gaya*, *Women Who Run With The Wolves*, *Gay Spirit Warrior*, and *Raising Psychic Children*. What's more, if you visit the place you're almost certain to meet grown women who believe in fairies and men (often with beards) who think nothing of holding long involved conversations with the local flora.

ROVING REPORT

A couple of years ago I visited the Findhorn Foundation on a one-day 'induction course'. This induction involved sampling the life of The Foundation in their large garden (I dodged out of the opportunity to also take part in the communal meditation). In the garden, five waiting Foundation members asked us to join a circle and to 'consider' and 'bless' the work we were about to do. There was a particular handgrip we had to adopt, holding the other hand right up to the thumb.

I began to feel uncomfortable; a feeling that wasn't helped when the woman who seemed to be in charge asked the regulars to 'tell everyone' what they intended to do and whether they wanted help from me. They all said that they preferred to work alone.

So the woman took charge of me herself, getting me to tie bamboo rods to rows of dahlias to provide protection from storm winds. I quite enjoyed it, even if I was slightly discomforted by the way the woman thanked each weed as she pulled it out of the ground. 'I like to let them know how they're not unappreciated,' she explained.

I enjoyed being in those pleasant surroundings. There were glasshouses full of huge beans, tall thick-leaved plants already weighed down with tomatoes, rich brown plots of earth full of bright-green potato flowers, huge floppy onion stalks, garlic bulbs, parsnips and carrots. Gigantic compost heaps, as big as sheds, mouldered away in four carefully segregated piles, looking as dark and smelling as rich as the finest fruit cake. Early summer flowers brightened every corner. It was, as everyone kept repeating, 'a good place to be'. They said that when they weren't saying, 'Welcome to Findhorn' in an oddly deep voice, anyway.

At the end of the session, we made another circle and were asked to 'examine our hearts' about what we had learned and how our 'bodies had changed in the garden'. I cringed mightily, but really, there wasn't much to complain about. I wasn't pressured to join anything afterwards and there were no hidden costs on top of my camping fee and the money I'd already paid. To my surprise, I'd found it a fun – and perhaps even enlightening – experience. And as the fighter planes from the nearby RAF base boomed overhead, I reflected that although The Findhorn Foundation may have seemed daft, it probably wasn't half so silly as the world outside.

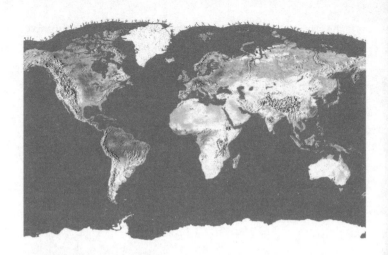

The Flat Earth Society
Founded: 1892.
Country of origin: UK.
Gods and guiding voices: 'God'.
Membership: Last recorded in the US in 1990 at around 2,800.
Texts: The Bible; Samuel Birley Rowbotham: *Earth Not A Globe*; Samuel Birley Rowbotham: *Zetitic Astronomy*.
Basic beliefs: The Earth is flat. God says so.

Are you really sure that the Earth is a globe? Do you have real scientific knowledge to back that up? Or are you blindly believing in Scientific Truth and taking all that stuff about Foucault's pendulum and measurements of curvature on trust?

Flat Earth theorists would say that if you are taking it on trust, you've been fooled. Nearly all ideas that support the Earth's 'globularity' are, in fact, contrary to reason. People that say they know that the Earth is round because ships have sailed around it are just displaying 'wretched logic'. After all, ships can sail around the Isle of Man and that doesn't prove that it's a globe. It's 'absurd' to believe that there are people living in the so-called Antipodes. Wouldn't they just fall off? And don't say they're hanging on because of gravity. What is gravity? Is it solid, liquid or gas? Have you ever seen it? Didn't think so. Do you subscribe to the theory that the Earth is rushing through space at the awful rate of 63,000 miles an hour? If you do, why haven't you been whirled off into space?

Flat Earth theory isn't a recent phenomenon. It's as old as, well, the Bible. That's the source of phrases like 'the four corners of the Earth', and that's why Christians suppressed Ancient Greek mathematical proofs for the roundness of the globe during the Dark Ages. However, from the ninth century onwards, the fiercest debates were not about the shape of the Earth, but its position in the universe. Galileo was imprisoned for saying the Earth went around the sun. Nobody really objected to the fact that he also thought it was round. It wasn't until an English gentleman, Samuel Birley Rowbotham, published his book *Earth Not A Globe* in the mid-nineteenth century, full of logical arguments like those printed above, that the shape of the Earth once again turned into a burning issue.

A six-mile stretch of canal called the Bedford Level became the scene of fraught experimental showdowns between the 'Flat Earthers' and 'globularists'. One convert to Rowbotham's cause, John Hampden, offered £500 to anyone that could prove him wrong. When Alfred Wallace did indeed prove that the Earth was round in an experiment conducted on the canal in front of impartial judges, Hampden called him a 'knave, liar, thief, swindler, imposter, rogue and felon'. He dedicated a large part of the rest of his life to writing poison-pen letters to Wallace and his wife.

In spite of Hampden's lost bet, Flat Earth Theory continued to thrive. Christians all over the world began to form societies attracting thousands of members. The original British Flat Earth Society was founded in 1892 and kept on going strong until the early 1970s when its last active members, Samuel and Lillian Shelton, died. The pictures of the round Earth taken from space had proved to be something of a crushing blow – although the society did come up with the rather neat explanation that the entire space programme was a con, and the moon landings were scripted by none other than the mischievous Arthur C Clarke.

There are still plenty of Flat Earthers in the US. They claim (logically enough) that creationists and other Biblical literalists are hypocrites for insisting that the Bible disproves the theory of evolution, but failing to also maintain that the Earth is, 'as God says', flat.

The Garbage Eaters, AKA The Brethren.
Founded: 1972.
Country of origin: USA.
Gods and guiding voices: 'God'.
Membership: About a hundred.

The Garbage Eaters are a nomadic group formed in the early 1970s and mostly made up of intelligent graduates recruited on campuses. They roam about the cities of the USA and Europe eating out of rubbish bins to press forward their message of anti-materialism. They call this 'dumpster diving'.

They take orders from Jim Roberts, AKA Brother Evangelist, a former US marine who preaches strictly from the King James version of the Bible, as all the others are 'corrupt'.

The men grow their beards long and wear long robes (slit up the side for ease of bike riding). The women never cut their hair. Smiling is frowned upon. Until quite recently, none of them were allowed to wear glasses and they considered going into libraries a carnal practice.

If you meet one, be on guard.

The Gentle Wind Project

Founded: 1983.
Country of origin: USA.
Gods and guiding voices: Benevolent spirits.
Membership: No figures available.
Basic beliefs: A nonprofit world healing organisation.

The Gentle Wind Project's aim is to eliminate so much suffering that they will ensure a better future for the entire human race. They intend to do this using a collection of 'healing instruments' engineered by the group's leader John Miller and inspired by his telepathic communication with 'nonphysical entities' or 'spirits' that live outside the Earth's physical and astral systems.

The organisation say that an invisible sphere around five-feet wide and nine-feet high surrounds each and every one of us, made up of 32 different levels of subatomic 'spiritual tennis netting'. This netting can be damaged by pain, fear and loss, but holding a healing instrument near it in the correct way should repair it. The instruments are generally brightly coloured. Some look like hockey pucks, some are cards covered in complex diagrams and pictures, and some have nifty spinning wheels on the end. According to Gentle Wind Project literature they can contain combinations of cell salts, herbs, and sometimes gold and other precious minerals. They work in a way too complicated for most humans to understand. The technology is based on a science known as 'radiational paraphysics' (sadly, there don't seem to be any university courses on this quite yet). When in use, the

HOLY SMOKE!

WHAT THE PUCK?

Professor David Touretzky, a research professor at Carnegie Mellon Univeristy, took apart one of the Gentle Wind Project healing instruments designed by benevolent space aliens communicating telepathically with the organisation's leader John Miller. Instruments like these can be obtained from the GWP website for a 'donation' of around $500. Here's what Professor Touretzky discovered:

- There's not much to it.
- The top is a piece of clear plastic. This is used to cover a piece of paper with an art design printed on it.
- The clear plastic cover is screwed to a ½-inch plain white acrylic disk.
- The bottom of the white acrylic disk has a hole to hold a small amount of sand (see photo). The sand is then covered with a blob of glue or epoxy placed on the

instruments are controlled telepathically by the talented headman, John Miller.

The Gentle Wind Project suggests that the instruments can help cure disease, return a sense of wellbeing, improve relationships with others, alleviate trauma, combat addiction, reconnect humanity into the world of benevolent spirits ... It's a big list, and you'd be forgiven for thinking that the instruments will have a correspondingly impressive price tag. Not at all. As the Gentle Wind Project readily points out, they are a not-for-profit organisation. The instruments are in fact free to use. If you can find an 'instrument keeper' you can use their healing equipment as often as you like. It's only if you want to benefit humanity and become an instrument keeper yourself that you're in any danger of parting with money. Then the suggested donations for each instrument ranges from $250 for an Advanced Family Unity / Integrated Space Set Card, right up to $7,700 for a New World System V.22.

To prove how eager they are to use the special instruments for the good of humanity, not for money, the Gentle Wind Project took a number of their instruments over to Southeast Asia after the catastrophic 2005 tsunami. They adorned their website with pictures of tiny wide-eyed children gripping Gentle Wind Project healing cards. They emphasised that they weren't showing these pictures to take advantage of the suffering to promote themselves. Not at all. They just wanted to demonstrate how effective the instruments are.

In spite of this charitable work and their many declarations of good

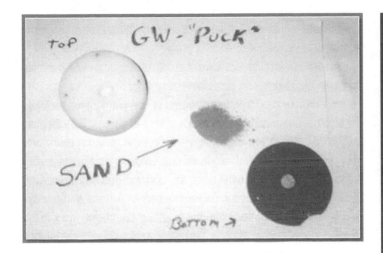

plastic bottom piece, to fit over the hole.
- The green plastic bottom piece is ³⁄₁₆-inch thick and is screwed to the white acrylic. It breaks easily when unscrewed; notice that a chip is missing in the photo.
- The sand is just that – a sandy substance with a slight smell of kitchen spice. No 'precious stones' uncovered, although the catalogue claims that these instruments include such stones.

It's possible to conclude, therefore, that the 'puck' must work by magic. Professor Touretzky says, however, that: 'The fact that this little band of crystal fondlers have been able to scam so many people is a depressing commentary on the state of science education in the US today.'

With thanks to David Touretzky: http://www-2.cs.cmu.edu/~dst/

intentions, the group has attracted a number of fierce critics. These detractors wonder why the 2002 Gentle Wind Project tax returns showed upwards of $800,000 being given over to 'education and research'. Surely this is a bit costly considering that the design specifications are provided gratis by spiritual beings. These nay-sayers have also had the temerity to question the collections of large houses and desirable cars that group leaders have amassed – or at least seem to have available for regular access. (Strictly speaking, members have given up all possessions.) The hostile cynics make the whole thing look more like a scam designed to bilk desperate and vulnerable ill people out of their money rather than a laudable attempt to heal the world.

Some bitter former members of the Gentle Wind Project hierarchy have even launched personal attacks against John Miller. Among their accusations are sordid allegations that John Miller encouraged female members of the group to participate in 'energy work' to help charge up the instruments. They say that this energy work involved Miller having sex with various women (often at the same time). They also say that Miller came to have a huge controlling influence on their lives. They lament that they became so dependent on the telepathic readings Miller could channel from the spirit world that they turned to him and his partner Mary for decisions about all aspects of their day-to-day existence. Right down to the small details. So everyone in the group became Boston Celtics basketball fans. They cut their hair short. They fed their pets the same way. They bought super gasoline rather than regular. Curiously, several people in the group have also renamed themselves 'Miller'.

Naturally, these allegations are hotly contested by Miller and his supporters. There are 'NO MESSIAHS' at the Gentle Wind Project, they declare on the website.

There isn't even anything to believe in.

Hermes Far Eastern Shining
Founded: 1997.
Country of origin: Tasmania.
Gods and guiding voices: Powerful water.
Membership: 300–400.
Basic beliefs: Buy our powerful water!.

Before they changed their name to Hermes Far Eastern Shining this group had the even more poetic name of Infinity Forms Of Yellow Remember. The new version was introduced not long after they fell foul of trading laws in Australia, when it was discovered that the bottles of water Infinity Forms Of Yellow Remember were selling as a

81

miracle cure for drug abuse, cancer and heart disease were just ordinary distilled water.

A 50ml bottle retailed at $80Aus – a mark-up of 400,000 per cent on normal Sydney water. That's an awful lot to pay, even if each bottle did have great titles like Heart Spider, Puff the Magic Dragon, Pharmaceutical Elixir, Agent Orange, Popeye's Spinach, Fiery Exorcism of Death Psychology and Don Juan Egg Elixir.

Infinity Forms Of Yellow Remember also sold pendants, body products and a device called a Saturn Bubbler, retailing for around $7,500 and described on their now defunct website as a 'vast' energy configuration made of rotating energy spheres that revolved around each other in an 'unfathomable' multidimensional array. (No, I don't understand either.)

The company director was a charismatic Antipodean who was once known as Gerald Attrill, but changed his name to Jessa O'My Heart (other directors were called Lightly Tossing Sunlight and Quantum Leaps). Intriguingly, Jessa O'My Heart's devoted followers are said to have been seen carrying around 'wands' of empowered water to protect themselves and gain strength. They even used to tap the wands against cups of coffee to take away the dangers of the caffeine.

Australian authorities said Infinity Forms Of Yellow Remember sold thousands of bottles of the special water before they had their run-in with trading standards officers. The minister for fair trading, John Watkins, described them as 'the old sideshow spruiker selling the cure-all elixir', and said: 'It's a mean con trick aimed at the most vulnerable people in our society.'

Since the name change, they've managed to avoid similar controversy – and expand into the US, the UK and New Zealand.

Ho-no-Hana Sampogyo
Founded: 1987.
Country of origin: Japan.
Gods and guiding voices: The feet.
Peak membership: 30,000.
Current membership: 0.
Basic beliefs: Feet are surprisingly powerful.

This Japanese foot cult became briefly famous in its native country at the end of the 1990s when a Tokyo court ordered its leaders to pay millions of yen in damages to former members. These victims had been told they could escape illness by giving the organisation large cash donations.

Ho-no-Hana Sampogyo, which roughly translates as 'teaching of the flower, three law practice', was founded by Hogen Fukunaga in 1987. He created a detailed personal mythology and theory of foot-divining; claimed to have healing powers; and said that he was able to see people's past and future by examining the soles of their feet. He once boasted 30,000 followers around Japan.

The victims alleged that after he inspected their feet, Fukunaga (don't say it too fast) told them they would get cancer and other fatal diseases unless they took part in expensive training sessions.

Known for his expensive suits and silver pompadour, Fukunaga led a lavish lifestyle from the foot-rubbing proceeds (estimated at up to ten million yen) and hobnobbed with world leaders like Margaret Thatcher and Pope John Paul II.

Then, in the year 2000, he was kicked into jail.

The House of Yahweh

Founded: 1980.

Country of origin: USA.

Gods and guiding voices: Yahweh.

Membership: Anything up to 3,000 live in the group's compound in Abilene, Texas, while thousands more subscribe to their magazine *The Prophetic Word*.

Texts: Yisrayl Hawkins: *There Is Someone Out There!*; Yisrayl Hawkins: *Why The Holy Garments?*.

Basic beliefs: Satan is a woman, the Pope is her prophet and the world was due to end in the year 2000, or maybe 2003, or at least in about three years. The Hebrew Bible texts contain a lot more information than people have realised ... The House of Yahweh have also published articles saying that the Russians have produced milk and coffee 'FROM ... BLOOD?!'.

Shortly before the millennium, the former rockabilly singer Buffalo Bill Hawkins (who has now changed his name to Yisrayl Hawkins) managed to convince some 3,000 people that he was a 'witness' who would announce Christ's second coming before being murdered by Satan and ushering in the end of the world in the year 2000. He and his followers hid out in an armed compound in scrublands near Abilene, Texas; a significant place according to Hawkins because, he says, if you travel west from the Abilene in Israel – the one mentioned in the Old Testament – you travel right though Abilene in Texas. This journey must be presumed to be miraculous as the two places are on very different latitudes. Still, the followers managed to build a 'holy

city' where they could await the End of Days. 'Thankfully, we only have a year left of this madness,' said Hawkins in 1999.

Of course, as it turned out there was more than a year to go. This didn't perturb too many of Hawkins's followers, however – several hundred of whom had already demonstrated their devotion to their leader by changing their own surnames to 'Hawkins' in 1996. They even stayed with him when he once again mistakenly prophesied that the last three years of mankind's time on Earth would commence in October 2000, when nuclear bombs were due to block out the sun and wipe out eighty per cent of the human race within twelve months.

By 2000, the faithful of the House of Yahweh had already become fairly inured to disappointment. Hawkins's long career as a uniquely insightful interpreter of Hebrew scriptures and leader of men is full of unfulfilled predictions. Soon after he first established his church, Hawkins had claimed his brother Jacob as a fellow 'witness' to the End Times. This dual project was scuppered when Jacob died of cancer. Even Yisrayl's attempts to resurrect the body as it lay in a funeral home had failed. Luckily, careful re-examination of the book of Isaiah revealed to Yisrayl that Jacob had been destined to die all along, while Yisrayl would survive as the lone witness.

Before this, Hawkins had also predicted that the Arafat/Israel peace

CULT HERO

BUFFALO BILL HAWKINS AKA YISRAYL HAWKINS

Yisrayl Hawkins has claimed that he is a Jew whose family was persecuted and forced to flee Europe for the United States. His parents, he says, can claim lineage to the tribe of Levi. A reporter from *Texas Monthly* explained this to one of Hawkins's brothers, who replied: 'Bill's my brother, but he ain't got both oars in the water, if you know what I mean. Our daddy was a Dutchman, our mother was three-quarters Cherokee, and we don't have a drop of Jewish blood in us.'

Quotes as originally published in the July 1997 issue of *Texas Monthly*.

treaty in 1993 would bring about seven years' tribulation, ending in The End (again in the year 2000). Mindful that the Scriptures promised a drought during the first three and a half years of the tribulation, the House of Yahweh began to stockpile food. Truckloads of wheat and edible goods were buried near the sanctuary in Abilene. This food quickly began to rot in ground made damp by winter showers. Word was spread around the compound that the Bible had actually promised an absence of *spiritual* rain.

Recently, Hawkins and his followers have also been busy buying property around Abilene with the money amassed from the tithes and donations gathered from the faithful over the years. He has restricted himself to saying that the most severe curses the world has ever witnessed will occur during the next three and a half years.

The International Society of Krishna
Consciousness, AKA Iskcon, AKA Hare Krishna.

Founded: 1965.

Country of origin: India.

Gods and guiding voices: Hare Krishna.

Membership: 5,000 worldwide.

Famous associates past and present: George Harrison, Allen Ginsberg (briefly).

Texts: *The Bhagavad-Gita As It Is*, translated by His Divine Grace AC Bhaktivedanata Swami Prabhupada.

Basic beliefs: By sincerely cultivating an authentic spiritual science, devotees are told they can become free from anxiety and achieve a state of pure, unending bliss. Each one of us is part of the all-powerful, all-attractive God Krishna. The most effective way for achieving God consciousness is to chant: Hare Krishna.

Words of Wisdom

" Philanthropists who build churches and hospitals are wasting their time. **"**

His Divine Grace AC Bhaktivedanata Swami Prabhupada

If nothing else, His Divine Grace AC Bhaktivedanata Swami Prabhupada was a master of timing. Had he started a daily routine of ritual chanting in a New York park at any other time than the mid-1960s he would probably have been ignored as a harmless, if unusually ugly, eccentric. As it was, he quickly became a worldwide phenomenon.

Prabhupada was 69 when he first arrived in America. He'd already had a successful career working as a manager in a Calcutta chemical plant and raised a family (which he'd abandoned when his wife burned some of his holy books). In 1965 he became convinced it was his life's task to spread Krishna Consciousness, a religion dating back to the sixteenth century when a Bengali saint, Chaitanya Mahaprabhu, founded an ascetic monastic order based on repeatedly chanting the name of the god Krishna.

Prabhupada set off in a boat for the most spiritually dark place on Earth – America – carrying little more than a pair of *kartal* cymbals, a suitcase and eight dollars. His fortunes began to improve when a group of well-educated hippies spotted him chanting away in the Tomkins Park in New York's Lower East Side and adopted him as their guru. Within a year he'd opened the first ISKCON centre, started publishing a magazine called *Back To Godhead*, was feted by countercultural icons like Allen Ginsberg, and had appeared at fashionable events in Haight Ashbury alongside acid Messiah Timothy Leary and the rock group the Fugs – writers of the song 'Group Grope'. Over in England George Harrison helped produce a single called 'Hare

KRISHNA MEDITATING

Krishna Mantra', which reached number 12 in the UK charts, and when Prabhupada visited the country he was driven from Heathrow airport in John Lennon's white Rolls-Royce.

Soon Prabhupada's Hare Krishna monks were a common sight in the West's larger cities; easy to spot with their flowing robes, beatific expressions and shaved heads (with just a small lock of hair left to grow at the back in case the god Krishna ever wants to grab it and carry them off to heaven). Their distinctive chanting was heard from Oxford Street to Montreal: 'Hare Krishna, Hare Krishna, Krishna Krishna, Hare Hare, Hare Rama, Hare Rama, Rama Rama, Hare Hare' (O energy of the Lord, O all-attractive Lord, O Supreme Enjoyer, please engage me in your service). They touted books at international airports. Motorway bridges were adorned with the legend: 'Say Gouranga – Be Happy'.

All those smiling faces and that exuberant dancing belie a strict lifestyle, however. Adherents are forbidden to eat meat, fish or eggs. There is no gambling, no sex other than for procreation within marriage and strictly no intoxication. All recreational drugs, alcohol, tobacco, tea and coffee are prohibited. Members also wear a necklace with 108 beads, each representing the Hare Krishna mantra, which must be chanted in full. The complete set must be repeated a minimum of sixteen times a day (that's 1,728 Hare Krishnas – about two hours' solid chanting). Monks who live in the temples rarely manage more than six hours' sleep on hard floors. Women (described by Prabhupada as 'prone to degradation, of little intelligence and

Cult Hero
THE GOD KRISHNA

Unlike the monks who so fervently chant his name, the Hindu God Krishna was not into self-denial. The Vedic legends portray him rather as a blue-skinned, four-armed flute-playing trickster. He hides the clothes of women bathing, he encourages married women to play around with him in the moonlight, he expands himself into 16,000 different forms so he can marry 16,000 princesses at once – and fathers ten children with each of them. One of his many incarnations also spends its whole time snoozing.

untrustworthy') are subservient to men. Adherents are encouraged to relinquish close family ties.

Still, until Prabhupada's death in 1977, the movement went from strength to strength. But soon after, it was engulfed in scandal. Eleven devotees were appointed to act as successors to the old guru, and put in charge of various international regions. Several of them proved to be wholly unsuitable. In West Virginia, for instance, Keith Ham was given a thirty-year jail sentence in 1987 for racketeering, mail fraud and conspiracy to commit murder after two bodies, partially dissolved in acid, were discovered in the creek near his commune. Handsadutta Swami, the man in charge of the northwest of the US and parts of Southeast Asia, hit the press after developing a taste for fast cars and hoarding weapons. The leader in London, James Immel, was dismissed from his post in 1986 amid accusations of drug abuse and sleeping with female disciples. His headless body was discovered not long afterwards in a shop called Knobs and Knockers on Regent's Park Road. Next to it, the police discovered one of his former disciples, sitting with Immel's severed head in his lap and muttering, 'The beast is dead.'

More recently the organisers have tried to concentrate on ascetic saintliness and put the mistakes of what they call 'the bad old days' behind them. Fortunately, they're nowadays far more likely to be seen spreading Krishna's love by feeding homeless people, selling books (by the year 2000, they claimed to have sold more than 450 million) or banging tom-toms than to be caught stabbing each other (yes, that happened too).

Words of Wisdom

6 The word "guru" means heavy. **9**

His Divine Grace AC
Bhaktivedanata
Swami Prabhupada

A Silly Old Cult!
Dr Gustav Jaeger and the science of psycho-osmology
Founded: 1885.
Country of origin: Germany.
Gods and guiding voices: 'Duft'.
Peak membership: 1,000.
Texts: Dr Gustav Jaeger: *Discovery of the Soul*.
Basic beliefs: Wool is good. You can capture the essence of soul in a ladies' hairnet.

In 1885, Dr Gustav Jaeger, a respected zoologist and early champion of Darwin's theories, published his two-volume *Discovery of the Soul*.

In it he claimed that the human soul was 'an odorous emanation' which he called *duft*. 'Smell,' he said, 'senses the soul.'

Ladies' hairnets, he discovered, were particularly rich in *duft* and he and his growing band of followers soon assembled a large collection. When Jaeger got hold of a hairnet from the head of a singer and placed it in water, he found that drinking the liquid improved his own voice. His wife's *duft,* meanwhile, he found to improve his reaction times. He quickly began a brisk trade in selling tincture of *duft* captured on hairnets.

Jaeger also maintained that emotion itself was caused by *duft* odours. Pleasant fragrances were beneficial, promoting cheerful, courageous and enterprising emotions. Unpleasant odours were harmful, causing gloom, idleness and depression. To allow the soul to breathe properly, and to maintain the beneficial odours, Jaeger recommended that people wear woollen clothes and sleep on woollen sheets and mattresses. Camel-wool was said to be especially effective at helping to preserve the soul and aiding weight loss.

When Jaeger died in the early twentieth century, his eccentric ideas went with him – but not before one of his followers had opened a shop in London under the name Dr Jaeger's Sanitary Woollen System. The resultant knitwear label bearing Jaeger's name can be seen on the high street to this day.

Jehovah's Witnesses

Founded: 1881.

Country of origin: USA.

Gods and guiding voices: Jehovah.

Membership: 6,000,000.

Famous associates past and present: Prince, Larry Graham, Serena Williams, Michael Jackson, LaToya Jackson.

Texts: The Bible (in the form of the New World Translation of the Holy Scripture).

Basic beliefs: Jesus Christ died on a stake not a cross. The End Is Nigh. After Satan's reign is destroyed 144,000 witnesses will go to heaven and reign alongside God. The remaining Christians will stay on Earth. There is no hell.

You can think what you like about the Jehovah's Witnesses, but you certainly can't avoid them. Around the world they're renowned as the people who put the 'piss' into proselytising and the 'off' into full-on fervour.

And while people may be rude to them when they go door knocking, the Witnesses themselves have an exemplary record of pacifism and politeness. Their determination, meanwhile, cannot be doubted. The vast scale of their missionary project is hard to even comprehend. Back in 1985, someone managed to work out that members of the organisation spent a combined 590,540,205 hours on house calls. A rough estimate of the number of houses they visit annually can be gained from the fact that they average 200,000 new recruits in a good year – and generally expect to convert one person for every 740 they

talk to. This means that they probably visit around 148,000,000 houses every year. In the same number-crunching vein, it's also worth mentioning that their huge New York printing press churns out around 100,000 books and 800,000 vividly coloured magazines daily. The semi-monthly magazine, *The Watchtower*, has a circulation approaching 26.4 million copies, making it by far the most widely distributed religious magazine in the world.

It's not surprising, therefore, that The Watchtower Tract and Bible Society of New York (as the Jehovah's Witnesses are formally known) is one of the fastest-growing religious groups on the planet. They have more than six million members, even though they've been around for less than 150 years and started on a very small scale when Charles

Taze Russell started a Bible reading group in the late-nineteenth century. Russell was a former **Millerite** who managed to come to terms with the Great Disappointment and the lack of Armageddon by predicting his own End Times, which he said were due to start in 1914.

Like the ill-fated Miller, Russell gathered a keen following – but failed to nail the correct date for the apocalyptic action. Since his death in 1916 the Society has had to modify its belief structure, for obvious reasons (some old adherents even left the group because they thought it had changed so much). Crucially, in the early 1930s, the society also adopted the name 'Jehovah's Witnesses', after a passage

Cult Hero

PRINCE

The pint-sized pop star and author of classic songs like 'Alphabet Street' and 'Sexy Mother Fucker' is one of the more unusual converts to the Jehovah's Witness organisation.

He's reportedly changed the lyrics to his hit 'Purple Rain' – adding a new line requesting that his listeners close their minds and open up the Bible. Still, while Prince may have changed from love-god to God-botherer, he's lost none of his old sense of style. The *Daily Mirror* reported that when he goes knocking on doors in Minneapolis he steps out of a limousine wearing a tailor-made suit, stack heels and mascara.

HOLY SMOKE!

UN-AFFILIATING FROM 'THE BEAST'

It's probably fair to say that the Jehovah's Witness faithful don't like the United Nations. In fact, they describe it as the 'scarlet-coloured wild beast' from the Book of Revelation and the very image of Satan's bloodstained political system. That's why members were so outraged when the UK's *Guardian* newspaper revealed in 2001 that The Watchtower Bible and Tract Society of New York had been secretly affiliated to the UN as a nongovernmental organisation for the last ten years. The same UN that they taught was 'a disgusting thing in the sight of God and his people'. The uproar following the article led the Society to disaffiliate from the UN almost immediately, causing some confusion at the international organisation. 'It's certainly a bit strange', said a UN spokeswoman. 'I guess we didn't know what they really thought of us.'

in Isaiah, which the group's own version of the Bible, The New World Translation, renders: '"You are my witnesses," is the utterance of Jehovah.'

Since these innovations, the Witnesses have developed into a strict apocalyptic fellowship, who run their lives according to how they think Christians lived in the first century AD. They believe that Jesus died on a big stake instead of a cross, they don't celebrate Christmas, and they say that only 144,000 elected Christians will go to heaven after Armageddon. Other good Christians will get to stay on Earth after The End, but the rest of us will become 'birdseed' as our corpses are pecked bare by crows. Most controversially, many Witnesses believe that the Biblical prohibition on drinking blood extends to blood transfusions and organ transplants. Hundreds of Witnesses (and their children) have died over the years after refusing life-saving operations.

The thing that rarely gets mentioned when the papers run stories on Jehovah's Witnesses who are facing death after rejecting blood, is that the alternative for them is equally grim. If they were to accept the transfusion, they would face the awful prospect of being expelled from the society of their peers. This process is known as 'disfellowshipping'. It's when members of The Watchtower Society are systematically shunned for breaking its strict moral code and failing to repent. Even family members sometimes refuse to speak to the lapsed individual. It's a tough penalty, especially since Witnesses are generally discouraged from mixing with outsiders (when they aren't trying to convert them). They often have no friends or family to turn to other than those within the faith. And it isn't just accepting blood transfusions that can bring on this horror. Reasons put forward in the past have even included reading books published by ex-members, eating with suspected dissenters and – harshest of all – wearing trouser suits.

Famously the Jehovah's Witnesses also preach that The End is coming – and we had all better get ready for it if we don't want to be birdseed. This belief is based on the prediction that the Earth's history is only due to last for 6,000 years after the creation of the first man, Adam. According to the calculations they've made from the genealogies listed in the Bible since Adam's time, the 6,000 years are almost up. We could all be in an awful lot of trouble. Luckily, there is a chance they might be wrong. After all, Jehovah's Witnesses have already predicted in the past that the End Times would arrive in 1914, 1918, 1920, 1925, 1941, 1954 and 1975. Nowadays they prefer to restrict themselves to 'very soon'.

The Jesus Army, AKA Jesus Fellowship Church
Founded: 1969.
Country of origin: UK.
Gods and guiding voices: 'God'.
Membership: 2,500.
Basic beliefs: Jesus rocks!.

Christians rarely seem to succeed when they attempt to be contemporary and 'get with' youth culture. Christian Rock doesn't work. Cleaned-up Christian hip-hop is insipid. Christian raves don't bear thinking about. Nothing compares, however, to the sheer embarrassing spectacle of the Jesus Army and their mobile sound system in full effect. If *they're* running the parties in heaven …

Over the last couple of decades the Jesus Army have become an increasingly common sight in Britain's cities, driving around in their brightly painted battle buses (often modified so they can pump out nerve-shredding Christian music at the drop of a Kangol hat), or marching down the street, crew cuts in place, wearing their distinctive red and blue combat jackets and sporting badges with legends like 'When you meet in the street, give the greet. Say JESUS! No shame, say his name.'

Also known as the Jesus Fellowship Church, the Jesus Army looks like a cruel satire of 1990s dance culture, but they're a deadly serious orthodox Christian organisation. They're particularly active in recruiting homeless young people, prisoners and ex-prisoners, and those involved in alcohol and drug abuse. It's this hard-sell missionary

work among the vulnerable that has attracted the most criticism. Detractors say that such gutter conversions are akin to men persuading drunk girls to sleep with them. The Archdeacon of Northampton (the town of the organisation's main headquarters), Bazil Marsh, has described the Jesus Army as being more like a 'snatch squad' than a church.

In the 1980s there was even more controversy thanks to a number of mysterious deaths and suicides among members of the group. Fortunately, there's been less of that recently, although in 2004 a member was jailed for trying to beat 'the devil' out of his son. Even so, in spite of recent attempts to improve their public image, many of the group's practices still seem uncomfortably extreme. Life in the Jesus Army can be tough. Alcohol is frowned on, and television has no place in the spartan communal houses. They don't celebrate Christmas. Adherents are requested to give up their possessions to a common purse. Men must ask 'elders' for permission to marry. Women, meanwhile, can't become elders and are generally responsible for domestic chores. Their strict adherence to biblical teaching has also created a repellent strain of homophobia. The Jesus Army claim to 'love' homosexuals, but try to teach them that they can learn to 'love naturally' and get married. The irony of this cruel stance won't be lost on anyone who has seen these camp Christian soldiers on parade.

ROVING REPORT

On the morning of 1 May each year, the students and townspeople of Oxford traditionally go mad. Just before dawn they all congregate (drunk) around Magdalen College, where, as the first rays of sunlight hit the ancient tower, choirboys start singing.

When this ceremony is over, all hell breaks loose.

When I was there in 2005, it was carnage. The drunkest revellers attempted to jump off the nearby bridge (which is about forty feet high) into the four feet of stagnant, shopping-trolley-filled water below. Forty people were hospitalised, several of whom had first torn open their limbs on the railings put in place to stop them climbing over the parapet above the river – and then jumped anyway, spraying blood into the dawn air as they fell, and inevitably incurring yet more injuries when they landed.

It was a hectic scene and by 8 a.m. there were an awful lot of damaged people wandering around. Even those who weren't covered in blood were ashen-faced, loose-limbed and slack-jawed. They looked like they'd just come back from a catastrophic battle rather than a night on the tiles. They were utterly defenceless against any assault – mental or physical.

So I wasn't surprised to see members of the Jesus Army striding around, pouncing on the most troubled.

'What do you think about God?' they were asking people who couldn't even remember their own names, while simultaneously glaring at the (and I quote) 'filthy pagan' May-Day morris dancers. The crowd was so thick that I was generally buffeted away from any encounters and it was only by chance that I came across another Jesus Army swoop much later in the morning.

By this time, I was feeling more than a little under the weather myself. I was trudging home

behind a man who was so far gone that he was unable to light his cigarette and was having serious trouble negotiating his way past street furniture. I was just noticing how torn and frayed his trousers were, and how old his shoes, when two multicoloured jackets appeared from nowhere and two Jesus Army soldiers forced the man to stop his inebriated progress.

'How are you brother?'

The two men hemmed him in against a wall, using a large wooden crucifix to block off any escape.

'Mmmmghha.'

'How do you think your life is going?'

Their close-cropped heads were pressed right into his.

'Mmmmghhha.'

'I've got some good news for you.'

One of the God squaddies suddenly raised both arms so quickly that the drunk flinched back in fright.

'Mmmmghha … Mmmmghha.'

I couldn't think how to react. I had been snapping some photos, which seemed to annoy the God men. I moved further back. Fortunately, they turned the other cheek and concentrated on their now very confused and helpless-looking target.

'Let me tell you about Jesus.'

This didn't seem like a request. It was an order. The man was now having trouble standing, but one of the Jesus Army men was making him place his hands on the wooden cross, backing him into some bikes as he did so.

'Jesus loves you!'

And so it began. Maybe I should have done something to intervene, but at the time, I reasoned that it would only make a bad scene worse and strip the man of yet more of his dignity. I cleared off just as the threat of hell came into play. I don't know if I did the right thing. I do know that I can't help wondering what happened next.

A Silly Old Cult!
Joachim of Fiore
Founded: *c.* 1170.
Country of origin: Italy.

In the late-twelfth century the Italian mystic Joachim of Fiore emerged from a long session of 'wrestling' with the book of Revelation to declare that he'd uncovered a hidden message stating that the Third Age would begin sometime between 1200 and 1260. During this Third Age every day was going to be like Sunday and the whole world was going to live in peace and idleness.

As 1260 drew to a close and the final catastrophe still hadn't occurred, Joachim's followers began to grow desperate. They took to savagely beating themselves with iron spikes, as they'd been informed that this would help bring the big day on. It didn't. Fortunately for Joachim there was nothing his irate (and rather sore) followers could do to avenge his mistake, as by 1261 he'd been dead for more than fifty years.

The Kabbalah Centre

Founded: 1969.

Country of origin: USA.

Gods and guiding voices: 'God', the Torah.

Famous associates past and present: Famous celebs who've been spotted wearing the sect's trademark red wool bracelet include Madonna, Britney Spears, Barbra Streisand, Jeff Goldblum, Roseanne Barr, Elizabeth Taylor, Naomi Campbell and Mick Jagger.

Texts: The Torah; The Zohar; Michael Berg: *Becoming Like God*; Karen Berg: *God Wears Lipstick.*

Membership: Not available.

Basic beliefs: The Kabbalah Centre claims not to be about religion, but about 'light'. The ancient wisdom of the Kabbalah can improve the world, they say.

Kabbalah has only started hitting the headlines relatively recently, thanks to the popularity of red bracelets among certain celebrities. Nevertheless, the website of the Kabbalah Centre claims that the belief has been around for thousands of years. In fact, they say, it's the 'oldest wisdom' in the world, as well as the 'longest' held secret and the 'deepest' mystery of life.

The society literature really does make Kabbalah seem incredible. As well as the oldest, it's the most influential wisdom in human history. Abraham, Moses, Jesus, Pythagoras, Newton, Shakespeare, Freud and the greatest minds of science, religion and politics wouldn't

HOLY SMOKE!

MONEY FOR OLD ROPE

Some prices from the Kabbalah website: Red string package: $26.00 (comes with a copy of Berg's *Red String Book*, as wearing the string is 'not enough' – you have to know why you've bought it) The Zohar (volumes 1–23): $415.00
Bead bracelet: $45.00
Incense burner: $22.00
Square glass anti-stress candle: $20.00
Meditation cards: $15.00 (they do offer connection to the infinite ...)
'Becoming Like God' Journal: $12.95
Stone (sustenance): $8.50 (they're 'empowered' with the 72 names of God)
Water holder: $7.95
Prosperity incense: $7.00

Interestingly, Judaism.com also sell their own anti-evil eye *authentic* Red String. You can get two that have been properly prepared – wrapped around the tomb of Rachel – for just $10. They're accompanied by a free CD.

contest this either. You see, they were all Kabbalah followers as well (whether they would admit to this, or even knew it, is sadly lost in the sands of time). Kabbalah does nothing less than reveal all the spiritual and physical laws that control the cosmos and the human soul. It can decipher codes! It creates order where there was chaos! It even answers the ultimate question of human existence! Small wonder that the Kabbalah Centre also claims that its methods can completely 'heal and transform' your life and alter the world 'for the good'.

The source of this mighty power is the Zohar, a set of ancient Jewish books that offer interpretations of the Torah (the first five books of the Hebrew Bible, or Old Testament). They're described by the Kabbalah Centre as being nothing less than the 'greatest force' of divine energy known to humanity – and the genuine holy grail.

The Zohar – or book of splendour – was regarded in traditional Judaism as so arcane that some rabbis advised that no one should even attempt to read it until they reached the age of forty. In the thirteenth century a branch of Jewish mysticism did develop around the Zohar, but it wasn't until 1969, when a former insurance salesman calling himself 'Dr' Phillip Berg got on the case, that the Kabbalah really hit the mainstream. He processed the Zohar and presented it in a readily accessible manner, providing a similar favour to 'ancient wisdom' to the one McDonald's does for cows.

Surprisingly, not everybody is grateful to Berg. The Chief Rabbi of England has issued an unprecedented public warning about the Kabbalah Centre, while the South African Chief Rabbi said, 'There have been cases of spiritual and psychological damage caused by the centre.' The Vatican has also placed the organisation on its watch list.

In spite of these doubters, the Kabbalah Centre continues to go from strength to strength. Even Michael Jackson was soon wearing a red string during his trial for child abuse in 2005. The Centre has also been doing a roaring trade in its special Kabbalah water. This success comes in spite of the bad publicity caused when an undercover BBC journalist Tony Donnelly – who was suffering from cancer – was offered cases of the stuff to help 'cleanse his cells'. His final bill for water, together with an equally useful set of the Zohar and a Shabbat (Sabbath) meal, came to a whopping £860.

The Latter-day Saints, AKA Church of Jesus Christ of Latter-day Saints, AKA Mormons.
Founded: 1830.
Country of origin: USA.
Gods and guiding voices: 'God', Mormon, Moroni.
Membership: 7,000,000 plus.
Famous associates past and present: The Osmonds.
Texts: The Bible; The Book of Mormon.
Basic beliefs: America was originally settled by people from the Tower of Babel. After his death on the cross, Christ made an appearance in America where he again preached the gospel. Indulgence in caffeine and alcohol is not good for you. Hard work is. The highest heaven is open only to baptised Mormons. The official church does not believe in polygamy any more.

In 1820, Joseph Smith, the founder and first prophet of the Church of Jesus Christ of Latter-day Saints, was confused about which of the many contemporary Protestant sects he ought to join. He solved his problem by asking God directly. 'None of them,' He said, appearing before Smith as a pillar of light. It was the first of many visions Smith was to receive in his lifetime.

Just over three years later, in 1823, another divine personage, an angel called Moroni, appeared by Smith's bedside. He was dressed in a white robe, 'his feet did not touch the floor', and he claimed to be the son of Mormon, the departed leader of an extinct American race called the Nephites. Moroni told Smith about a set of golden plates that contained a written history of the mysterious races that inhabited America before the time of Columbus. Then he disappeared to heaven in a shaft of light. A few minutes later Moroni reappeared at Smith's bedside. He repeated everything that he had just said, and then vanished, just as he had done before. Then he came back again and repeated the same words a third time.

Smith said that he didn't get much sleep that night. The next day he was understandably exhausted. He passed out when attempting to climb over a fence on his way out of a field – and the angel Moroni came to him yet again. This time he told him where to find the golden plates, buried in the side of a hill named Cumorah (near Palmyra in New York state). Smith went there right away and unearthed the famous plates. Buried alongside them was a pair of supernatural silver spectacles, the 'Urim and Thummim', which Smith was to use to translate the hieroglyphics on the plates. These were written in a language called 'reformed Egyptian'. (Curiously, archaeologists and Egyptologists say that there is no evidence that any such language existed.)

Smith spent the next four years preparing himself to do this great work of translation. Then he carried the golden plates home in a buggy (managing to get them there without anyone – not even his wife Emma – seeing them). He then set himself up behind a screen, so that the plates were still concealed, and got stuck into several years' hard graft.

A great deal has been written about the flaws in the resultant tome, the Book of Mormon (for more on this, see Appendix 3). It isn't just the inaccuracies and alleged plagiarisms that have offended the Book of Mormon's detractors. Its literary qualities are said to leave something to be desired, too. 'It is,' said Mark Twain 'chloroform in print.' The celebrated author of *Huckleberry Finn* also laid into Smith's habit of peppering his otherwise fairly contemporary nineteenth-century prose with biblical-sounding words and phrases like 'exceeding sore', 'yea', 'exceedingly glad', 'unto', 'great joy', 'harkening' and 'smiting'. If, said Twain, Smith had left out his favourite phrase, 'And it came to pass', then his 500-page bible 'would only have been a pamphlet'.

When the book was first published in 1830, it was savaged by the press. No reviewer seemed to have any doubt that Smith was a confidence trickster who had invented the whole story. Nor did Smith's personal life escape criticism. In 1834 an investigative journalist published a series of affidavits from friends and neighbours who described him as a lazy, untruthful, religious con man. They characterised the rest of his family as 'illiterate, whiskey-drinking, shiftless and irreligious'. They also suggested that it was no coincidence that Joseph's father, Joe Senior, was a persistent treasure seeker and that the young Joseph Smith had often accompanied him on his expeditions, hoping to find the loot left by Captain Kidd and indulging their fondness for the occult and fortune-telling on the way.

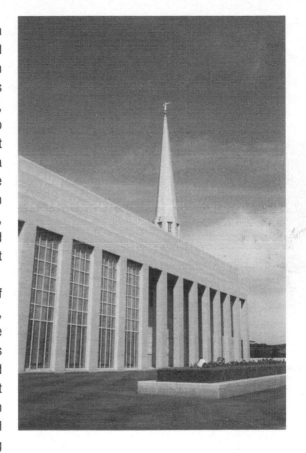

In spite of – or perhaps even because of – the negative publicity he was receiving, Smith soon gathered a considerable following. They gradually moved towards the less inhabited west of the USA to avoid religious persecution – persecution that only increased in 1843 when Smith declared that God had ordained plural marriage. A firm believer in practising what he preached, Smith was said to have gathered 27 wives by the time he died (some estimates put the number as high as 60).

Smith's death came in extraordinary circumstances, when a mob broke into the jail he was being held in, shot him and threw him out of a window. It was left to his successor Brigham Young to lead his followers on the long arduous trek across the deserts of Utah until they finally settled in Salt Lake City. There, safe from too much outside interference, the faith prospered. Brigham Young (also said to be a prophet – as are all presidents of the Mormon church) was a shrewd administrator and by the time he died the city was thriving. He had collected 140,000 followers and no fewer than 25 wives ('The only men who become gods are those who enter into polygamy,' he declared).

Since Brigham Young's time, the Mormon ideals of hard work and abstinence have paid off in abundance – as has the church's levy of a tithe on all of its adherents' incomes. Since officially abandoning the policy of polygamy in the 1890s (although several pockets of fundamentalists still exist who engage in plural marriages – outside the sanction of the church) the faith has become the apogee of American respectability. The Church of Jesus Christ of Latter-day Saints owns most of Utah, a large part of Hawaii and land in Canada, as well as the Marriott hotel chain, the Beneficial Life Assurance Company, and TV and radio stations. Its morally austere adherents have some of the lowest cancer rates in the US – and some of the best physical fitness. They promote the boy scouts, have short haircuts and the missionaries they send out around the world are scrupulously neat and remarkably polite.

Consequently, the religion is growing faster than any other in the US and spreading around the world at an incredible rate. What's more, in order to give those unfortunate enough not to be baptised into the Mormon church a chance of attaining the ultimate Mormon goal of divinity (they believe the most devout will get to populate their own planets), the Church is posthumously baptising thousands and thousands of people. If expansion continues at its current rate, by the year 5000, the entire world will belong to the Church of Jesus Christ of Latter-day Saints. Not bad, considering how it all began.

ROVING REPORT

The Church of Jesus Christ of Latter-day Saints is not a secretive cult. It's easy to get to talk to Mormons. In fact, I'd recommend it. If you're ever lost in a strange city, need directions and you see a street preacher with a short haircut, smart suit and black plastic badge declaring him an 'Elder', ask him. Chances are he'll speak excellent English, be scrupulously polite and he won't steal your wallet. It's a resource I've used on several occasions. Once, when I was in Basingstoke researching my book *Crap Towns*, an Elder was even kind enough to tell me that he would describe the town as being 'like hell'.

There's also a good chance that representatives of the church will come knocking on your door. The fiercely proselytising church sends thousands of young men and women out on missions all over the world each year. As luck would have it, a

'Negroes' are 'not equal' with other races, wrote Bruce McConkie, a church apostle, in his book *Mormon Doctrine* in 1966. The Latter-day Saints have since modified this doctrine, as they have the other embarrassing doctrine of polygamy, although this puts them in the difficult position of having to renounce the teachings of men they consider divinely inspired prophets.

couple of them came to my house just as I was starting to research this book. I asked them in for a cup of tea – forgetting, of course, that Mormons generally avoid caffeine. They politely declined, settling instead for glasses of water, and started to tell me the incredible history of the Nephites and Lamanites. They knew that the book is true, they said, 'through faith'. 'But,' they went on, 'there is also scientific evidence. In the pyramids "scientists" found a picture of a white god descending from heaven and teaching people. Therefore the Book of Mormon must be true.'

I was interested to learn that Mormon communities usually ostracised people who left their church – and that people only generally left it because 'they are lazy'. This started to make more sense when the young men described a typical day on their two-year ministry. They woke up at 6.30 a.m., exercised and studied until 10 a.m., knocked on doors for a few hours before having a one-hour lunch break, and then hit the streets again until 9 p.m. When they got home, they prepared for the next day. TV is strictly forbidden. 'We don't really know what's going on in the outside world,' they told me.

It's a tough routine, especially since most people just slam the door in their faces. The travelling Elders often also face violence. The young men told me about a friend of theirs who was chased through Crystal Palace with a blowtorch. Conversion rates can be depressingly low. Although a minister in the poorer, less literate regions of Africa can expect to perform up to 75 baptisms a year, most missionaries in Europe would consider themselves lucky to bring about a single conversion. Still, with 60,000 missionaries out and about every year, even this paltry success rate begins to be significant. Small wonder that the church is growing so fast.

MORMO BURN

Earnest and serious as the pale men sitting across from me at the table were, we never really reached an understanding. In fact, I got the impression that my persistent questioning began to freak them out. However, they left as politely as they came, giving me a copy of the Book of Mormon as they did. In it one wrote the instructions, 'Read. Ponder. Pray.' They certainly weren't your average twenty-year-olds.

A Silly Old Cult!
Klaus Ludwig and the Blood Friends
Founded: 1550.
Country of origin: Germany.

Sometime around 1550, Klaus Ludwig from Mulhausen in the Alsace region of Germany, proclaimed himself the son of God. He proceeded to teach the gospel of sex. His followers he called Blood Friends and they were initiated into his church by having intercourse with a stranger.

The church had one sacrament: rumpy-pumpy. Man was bread and woman was wine and when they made love, they performed Holy Communion. Children born within the church were considered holy and Ludwig taught his followers that they could not die. If a man felt desire for a woman, he was to consider it a message from God. If a woman was a member of Ludwig's church it was her duty to give herself up to any amorous male – whether or not she was married. At the end of each sermon Ludwig commanded his followers to 'be fruitful and multiply'. They stripped off, started up the sixteenth-century mood music and did their best to comply.

Ludwig, knowing something of the conventional morality of his times, also enjoined his followers to secrecy. Even so, the group was eventually discovered by civil authorities. Ludwig escaped, but three of his Blood Friends were put to death and the church was never heard of again.

The Manson Family
Founded: 1967.
Country of origin: USA.
Peak membership: 100.
Famous associates past and present: The Beach Boys.
Texts: Robert DeGrimston: *As It Is*; the magazine *Process*.
Basic beliefs: Christ and the devil have come together. To kill for the devil is a divine mission for the love of Christ – and Christ could well be Charles Manson.

Charles Manson scarred a generation. The murders he masterminded in 1969 helped destroy the hippy dream and ensured that no one would look at big-bearded dope smokers in quite the same way again.

If Manson had had his way in the first place, none of it would ever have happened. Shortly before the 32-year-old Charles Manson was released from jail in 1967, he'd begged to be allowed to stay inside. He thought he was permanently institutionalised, having spent more than half his life behind bars, on numerous charges, including cheque fraud, assault, pimping and rape. 'Oh, no,' he said, 'I can't go outside there …'

The world Manson returned to was very different from the one he'd left when he was last imprisoned. He emerged carrying little more than an old guitar and a book full of crazy songs, and wandered straight into Haight Ashbury, America's hippy capital, just as it was gearing up to the Summer of Love. Soon Charlie was indulging in LSD, amphetamines and free love. He was an attractive man, older than most of the other dropouts on the scene, and uniquely compelling in his rambling speeches about karma, loving the devil and understanding Hitler. He quickly gathered around him a devoted group of young women – who in turn brought in lusty young men. The Family was born.

There were always violent, racist underpinnings to Manson's teaching, but at first there was little to distinguish his commune of flower-children from all the others scattered around California at that time. In fact, to the casual outsider, all that drugs, sex and weird music looked kind of fun. Dennis Wilson from the Beach Boys certainly thought so. He let the Manson Family stay in his LA mansion in 1968 after he picked up one of Charlie's girls when she was out hitchhiking.

He even persuaded his famous band to record one of Manson's compositions, 'Learn Not To Love'. Less successful, however, was his attempt to get Manson a recording contract – a disappointment that is often seen as the impetus for the bearded wannabe Messiah's final descent into madness.

Wilson's association with the Family ended soon afterwards, when he took the drastic action of moving out of his own home and getting his manager to evict them. He estimated that they'd cost him more than $100,000 after he'd paid for the Mercedes they'd smashed up, a round of gonorrhoea injections, and the fact that they helped themselves to wads of cash. The final straw came when Charlie had threatened the nervous Dennis by waving a bullet at one of his friends, claiming it was a message and making dark hints about where it might end up.

Charlie and his freaky friends managed to find another place to stay when they persuaded someone to swap the small ranch he owned for a painted tent. (Unsurprisingly, the swap was made when all parties

HOLY SMOKE!

X-RATED

After Manson's arrest, Lynette 'Squeaky' Fromme, one of his toughest and most devoted followers, took over the running of the Family. With a handful of remaining females she took up residence on the steps of the Los Angeles courthouse during Manson's trial and shaved her head to protest at his conviction. Copying her hero, she even gouged an 'X' into her forehead, explaining later that 'We have X'ed ourselves out of this world.'

She was eventually arrested in 1975 after trying to assassinate the US president Gerald Ford. She'd managed to get close enough to him to shoot, but her gun jammed. She was heard complaining: 'It didn't go off. Can you believe it? It didn't go off!' before the police grabbed her.

were under the influence of LSD.) Soon afterwards, Charlie started sending his acid-fried minions on missions that he called Creepy Crawls: raids made on rich people's houses while the owners slept in bed. They took LSD to heighten their sensory awareness before sneaking into the mansions in total silence. Sometimes they stole valuables. Sometimes they just moved furniture around to 'freak out' the residents.

Manson's racist rhetoric also stepped up a notch. He became convinced that the Beatles were trying to communicate to him through songs on the *White Album*. The track 'Helter Skelter' foretold the reckoning that was soon to come.

Events snowballed. In July 1969 Manson shot a black drug dealer named Bernard Crowe in the chest after an argument over dope. Crowe recovered, but Manson became convinced that the radical Black Panthers movement would want revenge. The Family began to stockpile weapons and fortify their ranch. A week or so later, when Gary Hinman, a mescaline dealer and former friend of the Family refused to hand over all his money, they killed him. Then, at the start of August, Manson announced, 'Now is the time for Helter Skelter.' He thought that the best way to distract attention from his previous crimes – and get the Black Panthers off his back – was to start a race war. And, in his unique reasoning, the best way to start a race war was to start killing rich white people. It was, he predicted, going to be the worst hell on Earth. 'It will make Nazi Germany look like a picnic.'

On Friday 8 August, four members of the Family, Tex Watson, Linda

Kasabian, Patricia Krenwinkel and Susan Atkins, set off on an extra-special Creepy Crawl to 10050 Cielo Drive, Los Angeles, the home of a record producer, Terry Melcher, whom Manson had met through Dennis Wilson. Unbeknown to the Family, Melcher had sublet his house to the film director Roman Polanski. When they arrived, Polanksi was away in Europe, but his heavily pregnant wife, the actress and model Sharon Tate, was there, together with three dinner guests. They were all murdered, stabbed to death with savage ferocity. A young man called Stephen Parent, who had just happened to be passing at the wrong time, was killed as well, shot five times. Susan Atkins daubed the word 'Pig' in blood on the front door in an attempt to make it seem as if black radicals had committed the crime – and they left.

Continuing in the same vein of crazed logic that had caused this brutal slaughter, Manson thought an immediate follow-up was necessary. The next attack took place just one night later when Manson and seven other Family members walked into the bedroom of the wealthy middle-aged couple Leon and Rosemary LaBianca, tortured them and killed them. This time they carved the word 'War' on Leon's chest and wrote 'Rise', 'Death To The Pigs' and 'Healter Skelter' [sic] on the walls in blood.

The savage killings created a sensation. Sales of handguns and burglar alarms rocketed in Los Angeles and a huge manhunt began. Incredibly, however, the Family escaped arrest until October. Nobody is certain how many more people were killed in the interim. Manson

Words of Wisdom

' You say there are just a few? There are many, many more, coming in the same direction. They are running in the streets – and they are coming right at you! '

Charles Manson

was eventually discovered hiding in a cupboard under the kitchen sink at the Family ranch.

At the trial, Manson used the unusual defence that he and the Family were innocent because 'society' was guilty, a theme he has repeated at parole hearings ever since: 'You people have done everything in the world to me,' he said at one. 'Doesn't that give me equal rights? I can do it to you people because that's what you have done to me.' Naturally, this didn't hold much water with Manson's judges. Although he couldn't be directly physically linked to any of the killings, at the time of writing he remains incarcerated.

Jail has hardly diminished his influence, however. Charles Manson has made the transition from cult leader to cult icon more successfully than any other guru in history. In 2004 he was the subject of no fewer than three feature-length documentaries. His mad eyes stare out from posters, T-shirts, belt-buckles and even thongs. He receives more mail than any other prisoner in US history – more than 60,000 letters a year. He's even finally achieved his original ambition and had some success as a pop musician, with the likes of Guns N'Roses, the Lemonheads and Marilyn Manson all recording versions of his songs.

Matrixism

Founded: 2003.
Country of origin: USA.
Gods and guiding voices: The One, The Wachowski Brothers.
Membership: 500.
Texts: Andy Wachowski and Larry Wachowski: *The Matrix screenplays*
Basic beliefs: Reality is multilayered and 'The One' will come and bring world peace sometime between 1999 and 2199 – as predicted in the films.

Yes, this is a religion based on a blockbuster film. Matrixism started off as a spoof on the Internet, but now claims to have 500 genuine followers in the UK and America – and the number is rising all the

time. They use mescaline as a sacrament. They have four basic principles: belief in the prophecy of The One (that's Keanu Reeves in the film); acceptance of the use of psychedelics as sacrament; acceptance of the semi-subjective multilayered nature of reality; and adherence to the principles of one or more of the world's religions until such time as The One returns.

Becoming a 'matrixist' is unusually easy – you just have to go to http://www.geocities.com/matrixism2069/ and click on a link entitled 'join'.

I'm a member!

'You don't have do anything more,' acting secretary of Matrixism, Wendy X, told me. 'There are no dues to pay! However, it is important to spread the word about Matrixism around the Internet and elsewhere. You might consider it a rite of passage to hack something about Matrixism back into the Internet or society at large.'

I guess I've done my bit.

There is no information on how to leave.

A Silly Old Cult!
William Miller and the Millerites
Founded: 1818.
Country of origin: USA.
Gods and guiding voices: 'God'.
Membership: 50,000 plus.
Texts: The Bible.
Basic beliefs: Get ready! The end is nigh!.

After narrowly escaping death in the short war between the USA and Britain in 1812, William Miller dedicated himself to intense study of the Bible. Like many self-proclaimed prophets, he began to predict that the world was due to end (some time between 21 March 1843 and 21 March 1844). Unlike many self-proclaimed prophets, however, he was incredibly convincing. As the dreaded date grew near he amassed upwards of 50,000 followers, who all showed remarkable fervour.

Newspapers of the day reported that the Millerites – as they quickly became known – were giving away all their worldly possessions. Families had abandoned their homes, farmers refused to plant their crops. None of them would vote in elections. They said it was useless to elect a public official who was doomed to destruction before he could be sworn into office.

As the cutoff date for Armageddon of 21 March 1844 grew ever closer, the Millerites' activities became ever more frantic. Some began to climb up trees and onto the top of buildings so they could be

the first to see the descent of Jesus and be ready to ascend into heaven. One man strapped a pair of turkey wings to his back to aid his flight. Others carried umbrellas. In several towns local wags took to letting off trumpet peals. Millerites mistook these for the first announcements of Christ's imminent arrival and jumped off their perches in order to fly up and meet Him. The results were predictably painful – and often fatal.

By 22 March, of course, Miller was feeling somewhat sheepish. His condition wasn't helped by the popular press: 'WHAT! – NOT GONE UP YET? – WE THOUGHT YOU'D GONE UP! – AREN'T YOU GOING UP SOON? – WIFE DIDN'T GO UP AND LEAVE YOU BEHIND TO BURN, DID SHE?' taunted a Boston newspaper.

All the same, many of Miller's followers stuck with him. 'I still believe the time is not far off!' he said hopefully, and soon hit upon a new day to pray for: 22 October 1844. On the morning of the appointed day, thousands and thousands (some estimates put the figure as high as one in every seventeen persons in the US at the time) gathered on hilltops and the roofs of high buildings, arms outstretched as they waited for The Rapture. In the afternoon they were still there. By the evening they were getting tired. On the morning of 23 October they were apoplectic. There followed a mass nervous breakdown among the traumatised Millerites. The nonevent went down in history as the 'The Great Disappointment'.

Miller himself apologised. 'We were deluded by mere human influence, which we mistook for the spirit of God,' he admitted with refreshing honesty. He died five years later. Many of his apocalyptic beliefs lived on, however, in still-existing splinter groups like the Seventh Day Adventists and the **Jehovah's Witnesses**, who are both still convinced that The End will come pretty damn soon: so you better be ready.

Words of Wisdom

' Notice! As I am fully persuaded that the end of the world is at hand, and that in a few days the Savior will come in the clouds of glory, I offer my entire stock of goods, including ladies' and children's shoes, AT REDUCED PRICES! '

Advert placed in a New York shop

Morningland

Founded: 1973.
Country of origin: USA.
Gods and guiding voices: Donato Sperato (deceased) and his UFO friends.
Peak membership: about 2,000.
Current membership: about a hundred.

Morningland now appears to be an organisation concentrating on angels and New Age spirituality, but until quite recently, as well as being a multiservice sect dispensing tarot readings and Zen meditation classes, this Californian setup had a crucial line in Ufology – with particular reference to *Star Trek*. As a special feature, it used to charge people to cure them of AIDS. Sri Patricia, the group's leader and a self-appointed Messiah, also claimed that she could change people's DNA with the wave of her hand.

This cult has depleted in numbers over the past few years thanks to a series of sex, bigamy, murder and kidnapping scandals – as well as the death of its leading light Sri Patricia. At one point Sri Patricia (last names are banned in the group) had convinced thousands of followers to follow her to a fortified compound on Long Beach, California. There they raised hundreds of thousands of dollars, recruited more members through the favoured medium of yard sales, and waited for the return of Patricia's dead husband Donato – piloting a spaceship the size of Texas that was going to land on Long Beach (breaking a few space/time laws on the way) and take the Morninglanders away from the Earth.

Sri Patricia once said that after she died, 'the vortex would hold on its own for seven months'. After that, it would close and the presence of the Holy Father would give way to the destruction of the dark forces and Armageddon would ensue. She died in July 2003. That would put the date for Armageddon at 15 February 2004. It's pretty safe to say that she was wrong.

A Silly Old Cult!
Moses of Crete
Founded: AD 440.
Country of origin: Crete.

There was an ancient Jewish prophecy based on calculations made from the Talmud that the Messiah would arrive in the year 440. It seemed as though these predictions had come true – on the island of Crete at least – when a man calling himself Moses came forward and said he had been sent from heaven to lead his followers back to the Promised Land. Shortly, he was going to make the sea part and lead them through it, just like his ancient namesake.

When the appointed day came, hundreds followed Moses to a precipice overhanging the sea. He raised his arms, ordered the sea to separate and commanded his followers to fling themselves into the waves. Unfortunately, although dozens of followers obeyed him, the sea didn't. Those who jumped into the waters were dashed against the rocks and drowned. Moses probably perished along with them – at any rate, all accounts state that he vanished without a trace.

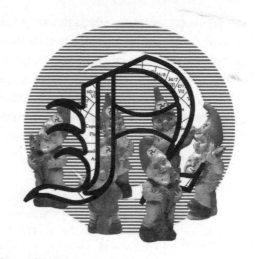

The Nation of Islam

Founded: 1930.

Country of origin: USA.

Gods and guiding voices: Allah, Muhammad, Elijah Muhammed.

Membership: Anything from 10,000 to 100,000.

Texts: The Koran; Wali Fard Muhammed: *Secret Ritual Of The Nation Of Islam*; Wali Fard Muhammed: *Teachings For The Lost And Found Nation in a Mathematical Way*; Elijah Muhammed: *Message To The Black Man.*

Basic beliefs: Once a radical variant on conventional Islam, declaring all white men 'devils' and with lots of stuff about spaceships, now increasingly conventional.

The Nation of Islam (NOI) isn't known for much in the UK other than its association with the renowned civil rights orator Malcolm X. The main reason that it's so obscure is that its leader Louis Farrakhan has been forbidden to enter the country because, in the words of the former Home Secretary David Blunkett, his anti-Semitic views are 'not conducive to public order'. So most people in Britain just tend to see the NOI as a radical political group with a racist leader and a nice line in bow ties, not realising quite how strange its origins and philosophy are.

The group was started in the black ghettoes of Detroit when a man called Wali Fard Muhammed appeared, seemingly from nowhere, peddling exotic silks and preaching a version of Islam based partly on the Koran and partly on a book he had written in his own symbolic language called *Teachings For The Lost And Found Nation in a Mathematical Way*. He declared that he wanted to teach the good people – black Muslims – about the evil whites and prepare them for the forthcoming battle of Har-Magedon in the wilderness of North America.

Fard didn't have long to carry out his mission because, sometime around 1933 or 1934, he disappeared without a trace. He left behind his charismatic disciple Elijah Muhammed. Muhammed believed that Fard was the God Allah in person and set about developing his teaching with devoted zeal, declaring implacable opposition to the white men and all their ways. These white men, he explained in his book, *Message To The Black Man,* were the result of a genetic plot.

They were created by Yakub, an evil scientist who had been exiled from Mecca and who wanted revenge on the authorities that had cast him out. The 'white devils' that he made ruled over the blacks for 6,000 years, but that dominion had ended in 1914. Now, the chosen of Allah were just awaiting resurrection from the mental death imposed on them by the white man. Elijah Muhammed claimed it was his task to bring about this resurrection.

In the late 1950s and early 1960s, it began to look as if Muhammed would have a chance of fulfilling his mission as his spokesman Malcolm X launched the Nation of Islam into the US national consciousness. However, disaster struck when Malcolm X converted to more conventional Islam and denounced Elijah Muhammed's segregationist views. Shortly afterwards – and, many maintain, not coincidentally – Malcolm X was assassinated.

The Nation of Islam gradually declined until Elijah died in 1975, his task seemingly unfulfilled. Then, Louis Farrakhan stepped in. He offered new hope for Elijah's followers, declaring that the old man hadn't perished – he'd just passed on. Now and again, he still flew to Earth aboard a gigantic flying saucer from where he issued Farrakhan with instructions. For a while, the society's paper, *The Final Call,* began to read like Funkadelic album sleeve notes, with headlines like 'UFOs and the New World Order' and bizarre talk of alien beings. Farrakhan re-energised the religion, but his unpalatable brand of homophobia and several distinctly racist, anti-Semitic pronounce-ments did little to endear him to society at large.

More recently the ageing Farrakhan has seemed to embrace a more conventional form of Islam and even expressed regret about the mistakes of the past. However, as his recent associations with the notorious Unification Church and the Nation of Islam's bizarre association with Michael Jackson (the singer hired – and then quickly fired – them as security while awaiting trial on child-abuse charges) suggest, the old man has lost none of his talent for causing controversy.

New Acropolis
Founded: 1957.
Country of origin: Argentina.
Gods and guiding voices: The spirits of nature
Membership: 10,000.
Texts: HP Blavatsky: *Secret Doctrine*; Jorge A Livranga Rizzi: *The Spirits Of Nature: Gnomes, Fairies...*
Basic beliefs: The society aims to stop the ascent of the brute masses to power, and 'reopen the gates of the Mysteries', so that a new breed of super-Aryan man can take over the Earth.

The public face of New Acropolis in Britain could hardly be more respectable. In their solid, old-fashioned headquarters building in North London they hold a school of philosophy 'in the classical tradition', providing easily affordable lectures on subjects like 'Destiny, Fate and Free Will'. Their website, meanwhile, proclaims that their ultimate aim is no worse than an ideal of universal fraternity.

In other European countries, however, it's a very different matter. They've been denounced as an occult and neo-fascist organisation that performs 'secret rituals' in ancient temples and maintains a secret 'kung-fu army' highly trained in martial arts. Their ultimate aim is said to be to eliminate democracy – which, according to their founder Jorge Angel Livranga Rizzi, 'governs people who are in a subhuman condition' – and to generate a new race of superhuman dominators.

The truth is probably somewhere in-between these two extremes.

New Acropolis has often and forcefully denounced racism and even the use of anything that could be mistaken for fascist iconography, but rumours abound about its political involvement with Le Pen's hard-right party in France and similar groups in Spain. Several of their leading members are Jewish in origin, and their Argentinian founder Rizzi often proclaimed he wasn't anti-Semitic. On the other hand, he also had a marked fondness for giving the fascist salute and declared that he wanted to create a new Aryan race to rule the world. The less able, he said, would be 'left behind' and treated without 'false sentimentality'.

New Acropolis does use a lot of military terminology in its organisational structure and its Spanish branch did once run into trouble for hoarding weapons, but no large scale kung-fu army has yet been uncovered. Rizzi did also criticise democracy as a weak and unnatural system, but so far the group he founded seems to have taken no more radical action to bring about its downfall than holding philosophy classes and outward-bound weekends.

New Acropolis is, in fact, something of a mystery. Perhaps the best thing to do for anyone wondering about its true nature would be to read a book by Rizzi, its founder and guiding light. It's called *The Spirits of Nature,* it's dedicated to a small gnome who was a personal friend of the author and it provides advice on how to visualise elves and fairies.

ROVING REPORT

When I signed up for a course on Mind Over Matter at London's New Acropolis headquarters, there was a small part of me that hoped I was going to learn how to lift solid metal objects just by looking at them, and how to turn my enemies' hands to cabbages. Things certainly looked promising when I arrived in a candle-lit room, scented with incense and filled with curious statues, hieroglyphic wall tablets and arcane knick-knacks from ancient societies. The illusion was broken, however, when someone explained to me that the reason the hypnotic mystical music was being played on the stereo was that it was the only CD they could get to work.

The talk turned out to be a fairly dry, but nonetheless thought-provoking, hotchpotch of Oriental mysticism ('Eastern thinking') and psychotherapy. I learned that the best way to focus on a black dot was to shape my mind like a black dot, but that I wouldn't be able to do that for very long.

Or something.

Anyway, the talk was pretty inoffensive; even the stuff about 'shaping the future' seemed no more sinister than most company pep talks. It was the tea and cake that followed that really freaked me out. The cakes themselves were really quite pleasant, but it was the intensity with which they were pressed on me that made me feel uncomfortable. Each New Acropolis regular took it in

turns to talk to me, and each professed a profound interest in my personality. 'What did you think of the talk, Sam?' they asked. It was unnerving how they'd all memorised my name. Then they would launch into a series of probing questions about my beliefs, work and even where I lived. They seemed fascinated by everything I said. They really seemed to care about me.

In the 1970s, paranoid anti-cult activists used to see this intense and sudden affection as a specific indoctrination technique and called it 'love bombing'. I was unsure whether it was anything more sinister than a group of lonely people who were eager to make a new friend and to bring a new person into their gang. All the same, the attention began to unnerve me after a while, especially thanks to the eagerness with which they all tried to encourage me to come to the next gathering. I made my feeble excuses and left soon after someone offered me a third slice of cake.

I did manage to clear up the vexed question of the kung-fu army, though. I was told that New Acropolis do train their members (in countries where there are enough of them) in martial arts, but only to help their spiritual and physical development. They won't be troubling any democratic governments with them any time soon. At least, I don't think they will.

Opus Dei
Founded: 1928.
Country of origin: Spain.
Gods and guiding voices: 'God'.
Membership: 85,000.
Famous associates: Franco (murderous fascist dictator), Pinochet (murderous fascist dictator), Ruth Kelly (member of the UK Labour party).
Texts: The Bible; Josemaria Escriva de Balaguer: *The Way* (a collection of 999 meditations to help prayer).
Basic beliefs: Members should live their Christian faith in deed as well as thought.

Words Of Wisdom

❝ And she there has to be spanked throughout. Draw up her skirts, tear down her panties and give it to her in the ass!! In the ass!! Until she talks. MAKE HER TALK! ❞

A comment by Opus Dei founder Josemaria Escriva de Balaguer, in reference to a woman who had disobeyed him, as reported by the writer Carmen Tapia in *Beyond the Threshold: Life in Opus Dei*

The mysterious Roman Catholic sub-sect, Opus Dei, came to the attention of the world thanks to Dan Brown's bestselling novel *The Da Vinci Code*. In this book the organisation is depicted as a shadowy cult made up of sadomasochistic monks intent on killing their enemies, harming themselves with whips and taking over the world by discovering the Holy Grail. It's a portrayal that the Catholic Church has strongly objected to. Past masters at slamming the stable door after the horse has bolted, the Vatican issued a proclamation in March 2005 urging people not to read Brown's work and even gave the Archbishop of Genoa the job of debunking its ideas. By that time, of course, *The Da Vinci Code* had already sold over 18 million copies in 44 languages and was being made into a blockbuster film.

The Vatican says that Brown's fiction is full of 'shameful and unfounded errors' and, as a writer of thrillers, it's certainly Brown's prerogative not to let the truth get in the way of a good story. However, while his portrayal of Opus Dei may not be strictly accurate, there are many aspects of the organisation that have raised serious concerns among anti-cult organisations around the world – and created huge numbers of bitter, damaged ex-members.

These critics call it misogynistic, fundamentalist, and anti-modern. Opus Dei, meanwhile, denies that it is any kind of 'cult'. They say that the organisation is a forward-thinking arm of the Catholic Church and that they're flourishing in the modern world. If, they contend, they were involved in any cult practices they would have been suppressed by the Catholic Church and not encouraged by such luminaries as

Pope John Paul II. However, Opus Dei do admit that 'mistakes' have been made in the past.

'Opus Dei' means God's task. It was founded in 1928 by the Roman Catholic priest Josemaria Escriva de Balaguer, who wanted to encourage Catholic lay people to see religion as something that should direct every minute of their lives, rather than something they only paid

Cult Hero

JOSEMARIA ESCRIVA DE BALAGUER

Josemaria Escriva de Balaguer claimed that he received the monastic calling after seeing footprints left in the snow by a barefoot friar, near his home in Logroño, northern Spain. He established Opus Dei in 1928 in Madrid. His work was hindered by the outbreak of the Spanish Civil War, which prompted him to flee the capital until Franco's fascist junta was safely established there. He returned in 1939 and sided with the Franco government as it enforced its rule on his native country. The mass graves from that period are still being uncovered.

Later, Escriva moved to Rome where he gradually established himself within the Vatican hierarchy, occasionally taking trips to Latin America, where Opus Dei members became members of the government of Augusto Pinochet. The mass graves from that period are still being uncovered.

When Escriva died in 1975, Opus Dei was a large and thriving organisation. He was beatified by Pope John Paul II (a great admirer) in St Peter's Square on 17 May 1992, in front of over 200,000 people. Ten years later he was promoted to the rank of Saint, in front of 300,000 people. It was one of the fastest canonisations in history. The Catholic Church is adamant that the large donations made to its coffers by Opus Dei had nothing to do with this unusual speed.

attention to when they turned up for Mass or confession. Members are therefore expected to live holy lives, to try to convert people they know, and to observe daily religious devotions.

These devotions include 'corporal mortification'. Members are encouraged to take cold showers every day and observe several hours' silence. The more committed members, known as 'numeraries' (who make up about a third of the organisation) are given a *celice*, a spiked garter to wear around their thigh for two hours a day, and a whip to use on their own back and bottom. The Opus Dei constitution explains that these masochistic practices are 'for the purpose of chastising the body and reducing it to servitude'. Former members have additionally claimed that they were made to sleep on boards and forced to fast. Opus Dei says this is merely an example of Christian 'self-denial' although critics believe it goes beyond that.

Numeraries also agree to become celibate and to donate any earnings that they don't need for basic living to Opus Dei. Many former members claim that they parted with their entire income. Others have claimed that the group vetted all mail sent to numeraries, but these reports are dismissed by Opus Dei, who say that the practice stopped 'some years' ago.

One of the most chilling criticisms from former members is that they were forbidden to read all kinds of books – even many on the reading lists of Catholic universities. Opus Dei again have a different spin on this. They say that members ask for advice before reading a book, and they are free to reject it. All the same, this didn't stop the media furore in the UK when Ruth Kelly, a Labour MP closely associated with Opus Dei, was appointed as Education Secretary in 2005. When pressed, she refused to confirm or deny that she was a member of Opus Dei, saying merely that it gave her 'spiritual support'. She described her association with the book-proscribing, anti-contraception organisation as a 'private matter' that would not impinge on her work with Britain's universities and young minds.

Opus Dei is growing rapidly.

The Order of the Solar Temple

Founded: 1984.

Country of origin: Switzerland.

Gods and guiding voices: The Knights Templar, Joseph Di Mambro, Dr Luc Jouret.

Peak membership: 442.

Current membership: around thirty.

Texts: Luc Jouret: *Medicine and Conscience*; Luc Jouret: *Fundamental Time of Life: Death* (audiocassette).

Basic beliefs: A mixture of medieval mysticism centring around the fourteenth-century Christian order of the Knight's Templar mixed in with astrological New Age fantasy.

The Solar Temple gained worldwide notoriety because of an awful tragedy: 74 of its members were found dead in Switzerland, Canada and France between 1994 and 1997.

The Solar Temple was a group that had been operating for just ten years before the first deaths. In that time, its two leaders, Joseph Di Mambro and Dr Luc Jouret, had managed to attract an unusually powerful and influential membership body that included politicians, civil servants and police officers.

Di Mambro and Jouret created an alternative world for these followers, with secret masters and impressively staged night-time ceremonies where they wore robes modelled on Crusader knight's costumes. Di Mambro convinced members that he was a member of the Knights Templar during a previous life and that his daughter Emanuelle was a 'cosmic child', conceived without sexual intercourse. He carried with him a sword that he said had been given to him a thousand years before and he performed miraculous feats (which former members later denounced as conjuring tricks).

These strange rites were so powerful that none of the members seemed to doubt that they had special powers or that they would one day form a small elite destined to reach the star Sirius. The two leaders also managed to persuade their followers to part with large sums of money. They amassed a multimillion-pound fortune and property empire, as well as stockpiles of weapons. Some say it was squabbling over this money that led the leaders to such an extreme conclusion in 1994. Others claim that the group was actually a Mafia-involved organised-crime front that had fulfilled its useful purpose. Others still maintain that DI Mambro and Jouret genuinely believed they'd found the way to Sirius. Whatever the theory, the known facts are stark and horrifying.

The grim tale began around midnight on 4 October 1994 when flames erupted into the dark skies from the farmhouse of Alberto Giacobino near the small Swiss farming village of Cheiry (not far from Geneva). Firemen arriving on the scene first found Giacobino lying dead on a bed with a plastic bag over his head. He had been shot. Then, stuck on a door, they discovered an audiocassette, later found to contain a rambling astrological discourse. They moved into a partly ruined barn where they discovered a number of undamaged rooms, including a chapel with walls covered in mirrors and hung with red satin drapes. The floor was covered in empty champagne bottles …

and dead bodies. There were 22 in all, many cloaked in ceremonial robes. They were arranged in a star formation with their faces looking towards a makeshift altar, upon which there were a rose, a cross and a Christlike portrait of Jouret. Ten of the corpses had plastic bags tied over their heads. Several had their hands bound. Nearly all had been shot.

A further 25 bodies, including some children, were recovered in three burned-out chalets in Granges-sur-Salvan, 47 miles east of Geneva, near the Italian border, on the same night. Then two more bodies were found in an apartment belonging to Di Mambro's close associate, Dr Luc Jouret. Just over a year later, another sixteen bodies were found in a Swiss mountain valley known locally as the pit of hell. They had all taken the sedatives Myolastan and Digoxine. Most had been shot in the head. They too were arranged in a star formation. Finally, in March 1997, five more people died in Quebec.

Although conspiracy theorists claim that Jouret and Di Mabro are still alive, they almost certainly died in the first mass suicide in Switzerland. Their influence lives on, however. There are thought to be at least 30 surviving members in Quebec and a possible total of 150 worldwide. Police authorities try to keep track of them, but there's every chance that we haven't heard the last of the Order of the Solar Temple.

The Panacea Society

Founded: 1926.
Country of origin: UK.
Gods and guiding voices: 'God', Joanna Southcott.
Peak membership: 60.
Current membership: Less than five.
Texts: Joanna Southcott: *Sound An Alarm In My Holy Mountain.*
Basic beliefs: The secret to eternal bliss is inside a locked box. Only bishops can open it.

Joanna Southcott was one of the eighteenth century's most famous and enterprising prophets. Her apocalyptic anti-Semitic books were unfailingly popular (all sixty of them); she regularly drew huge crowds to meetings, where she would make dramatic predictions and fall into alarming fits, and her habit of publicly berating officials and churchmen ensured that she was never long out of the press.

Her fame reached its height in 1814, her 65th year, when she announced that even though she was still a virgin she was pregnant – with the next Messiah, whom she planned to name Shiloh. Unfortunately she died soon afterwards and a postmortem revealed that, rather than a bouncing baby Son-of-God, she'd been carrying around an ugly, cancerous growth. Her large band of followers didn't despair, however, because just before her death Southcott did manage to bequeath them a large sealed box, which she said contained no less than the prophecy of the millennium as foretold in the gospel of St John, and the secret to eternal bliss.

The box came with the instructions that it wasn't to be opened until a time of great crisis – and only then in the presence of no fewer than 24 bishops of the Church of England. That didn't stop the antiquarian researcher Harry Price taking a look in 1927, however, when he staged a public opening. He and the onlookers were surprised to find that the contents included a horse pistol, a lottery ticket, a dice box, a purse, some old books and, most enigmatically, a nightcap.

The story didn't end there, however. Soon after Price's exhibition, an ex-lunatic-asylum patient called Mabel Barltrop came forward to say that Price had opened the wrong box and that she had the original. What's more, she was the incarnation of Southcott's unborn child Shiloh ... and the bride of Christ. She also claimed that Armageddon

was imminent and that pretty soon Jesus Christ was going to come along and establish the New Jerusalem near her home in the otherwise unremarkable market town of Bedford (see photo).

Barltrop gathered together quite a following, known as the Panacea Society. They proved expert at raising capital and soon started buying properties around Bedford in readiness for the day when Christ came to take up residence.

In the 1970s the ageing society members ran an advertising campaign urging 24 bishops to get together and fulfil Southcott's prophecy. 'Crime and Banditry, Distress and Perplexity will increase in England until the bishops open Joanna Southcott's box,' they warned. Unfortunately no bishops came forward and the box remains

HOLY SMOKE!

TICKET TO PARADISE

The Panacea prophetess Joanna Southcott can lay considerable claim to having invented the phrase 'ticket to paradise'. She used to sell special stamped certificates (costing just 21 shillings and out of a limited run of 144,000) that enabled the bearer to stride straight through the pearly gates of heaven. When one of the tickets was found clutched in the lifeless hand of an executed murderess, their market value plummeted.

unopened. The bishops haven't even responded positively to a concerted letter-writing campaign. 'Really,' says one of the last surviving society members, Ruth Klein, 'some replies are quite rude.'

The society's houses are still ready and waiting for Jesus to move in, however. The increasingly elderly members have had a few anxious moments. They hesitated before installing a shower – unsure about whether He will have a radiant body and therefore not need conventional plumbing. The Lord's continuing no-show has been a bit of a strain too. Ruth Klein accepted the chairmanship of the society on the understanding that He would come in the year 2000. 'I thought, "I'll do this until the Lord comes and He will take over." I did think He would come, actually, but there we are. We plod on until he does.'

Hopefully, her disappointment was lightened by the knowledge that their wise property investments have ensured the Panacea Society a net worth of more than £30 million.

Ruth Klein quotes courtesy of Screaming Eye, the makers of the splendid TV programme *Maidens of the Last Ark*.

The Panawave Laboratory Group
Founded: 1977.
Country of origin: Japan.
Gods and guiding voices: Electromagnetic waves.
Peak membership: 1,200.
Current membership: Figures not available.
Basic beliefs: Electromagnetic waves cause catastrophic environmental destruction. Communists are bad. The world was supposed to end on 15 May 2003.

When fifty people wearing white coats and surgical masks took over a 660 ft stretch of mountain road in Gifu prefecture (about 200 miles west of Tokyo) and covered up roadside crash barriers and trees with huge white cloths, the local citizens were understandably confused. When the strange group refused to allow traffic along the road and then explained that they had to wear the white clothes and also cover their nearby fleet of vehicles with white sheets to protect their ailing leader (who was suffering from terminal cancer after communist guerrillas had attacked her with microwaves), the residents began to get annoyed. They erected signs saying GET OUT NOW! and a nasty standoff was only averted when the police moved on the white people and their vehicles because they were breaking traffic laws.

It was May 2003, and the mysterious people intent on covering things in sheets were representatives of Panawave, an organisation that had already gained some notoriety in Japan following a bid to capture a bearded seal that had appeared in a Tokyo river a thousand

miles from its arctic home. Panawave believed that the seal had been led astray by bad electromagnetic waves and wanted to return it to the icy northern seas. Sources said that members believed rescuing the seal would save mankind from 'certain destruction'. However, sympathy was lost for their well-intentioned actions when the group released a pamphlet saying that 'people without the ears to hear will all face death'.

Panawave were convinced that electromagnetic waves were causing terrible environmental destruction and, in addition, that communist guerrillas from the former Soviet Union were launching their own electromagnetic terrorist attacks. They'd been touring Japan since the mid-1990s in search of a place free from power lines and electromagnetic pollution, but by May 2003, they'd reached situation critical. The world, said their sick leader Yuko Chino, would be destroyed on 15 May when a previously unheard-of planet came too close to Earth's orbit and reversed the magnetic poles, thus causing great floods and tidal waves.

Shortly after they'd been moved on from their road in Gifu, the white-clad cultists appeared by a river in Fukui in central Japan and covered a long stretch of embankment with white fabric. Their hope was to protect themselves from electromagnetic wave attacks, but they were quickly moved on again by the police. On 15 May a spokesman for Panawave declared that the predicted doomsday might actually be delayed until 22 May. A week later, when it became clear that the world might just survive, the group disappeared from the media spotlight just as suddenly as they had arrived.

Cult hero

YUKO CHINO

Panawave leader Yuko Chino was an enthusiastic streaker in her late thirties. She was fond of running naked through her home town of Kyoto. She would do this regularly, letting it all hang out until her mother came and dragged her back home. In 1984 she is said to have married one of her followers – although they seem never to have met before the ceremony. The husband separated from her in the early 1990s, annoyed with Chino's obsession with dangerous electromagnetic waves. Soon after that she took to wearing a white tracksuit made of all natural materials and started refusing to bathe.

The People's Temple, AKA Jonestown.
Founded: 1953.
Country of origin: USA.
Gods and guiding voices: 'God'.
Peak membership: 4,000.
Texts: The Bible.
Basic beliefs: Hardline evangelical Christianity.

On 18 November 1978, the Reverend Jim Jones and 912 of his followers died at Jonestown, a 300-acre compound in the Guyana jungle. Many drank cyanide-laced Kool-Aid; others who tried to resist the mass suicide were shot – 276 of the victims were children.

Jim Jones had founded his Christian fellowship in Indiana, USA in the early 1950s, advocating and aiding social justice. His preaching stressed the need for racial brotherhood and integration, and his group helped feed the poor and find them jobs. As it expanded and moved to California in the early 1970s, the People's Temple was viewed by many outsiders as a model of racial integration and social action. Their charismatic leader, known as 'Dad', was regarded as a humanitarian leader.

Sadly, it soon became apparent that there were wide discrepancies between what Jim Jones preached and what he practised. A few people who had succeeded in leaving the cult claimed that Jones was stealing from his followers, that he faked miracle healings and that he now considered himself the new Messiah. They described a frightening hidden world where families were systematically divided, 'disciplinary' beatings were meted out with alarming frequency and fervour, and Jones's sexual exploitation of those around him – male and female – was a dirty open secret.

As the temple came under increasing scrutiny for these abuses as well as large-scale money laundering, the increasingly paranoid Jim Jones began to say that the authorities wanted to destroy him and his followers. In 1977, he sought refuge in the jungles of Guyana, taking over a thousand followers with him, telling them that they were going to build a socialist paradise, free from the pollutions of the outside world.

Instead, they found themselves in a fortified compound where 'wrong-doers' were placed in sensory-deprivation boxes and pits, where rations were low and where their increasingly tyrannical leader made them rehearse committing suicide together.

In November 1978, US Congressman Leo Ryan arrived at the Jonestown compound, intent on investigating the claims of abuse. Soon he had seen enough and decided to leave. A number of members of the Temple declared that they wanted to go with him. When they arrived at the local airstrip, they – together with Ryan and three journalists – were shot dead by Jones's followers. One of the journalists captured the shootings on film, before he himself was killed.

Back at the temple, Jones made a rambling speech over the PA system, recording his words on tape: 'I didn't order the shooting … I don't know who shot the congressman,' he declared. He exhorted his followers not to resist the poisonous drink being passed around in paper cups – or, in the case of babies and toddlers, a poisonous purple liquid, which was to be injected into their mouths.

'So you be kind to the children and be kind to seniors, and take the potion like they used to take in ancient Greece, and step over quietly,' Jones urged. 'We are not committing suicide. It's a revolutionary act.'

A woman can be heard on the tape challenging the decision to drink the cyanide. She was shouted down. Jones then told his followers, 'I don't care how many screams you hear, death is a million times preferable to spending more days in this life … No more pain. No more pain … That's what death is, sleep. Have trust. You have to step across. This world was not our home.'

Some survivors have said that there were guards standing around the perimeter, with orders to shoot anyone who attempted to leave. It's been claimed that only 200 of the victims died willingly. The other 700 were murdered.

In total, 913 people, including Jones, died that night. In one pavilion, eighty contorted bodies were discovered beneath a sign placed there in the days when Jonestown had seemed like a socialist utopia. The sign contained a quotation from the Spanish philosopher George Santayana. The words form a stark reminder of the continuing significance of this awful tragedy: 'Those who do not remember the past are condemned to repeat it.'

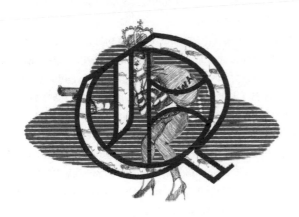

Queen Shahmia
Founded: 1991.
Country of origin: USA.
Gods and guiding voices: 'God', Queen Shahmia.
Membership: Fourteen.
Basic beliefs: Shahmia is the daughter of God and Jesus Christ's queen.

In early 2000, Fort Myers in Florida was hit by a series of armed robberies. The same outfit of burglars were seen on the CCTV cameras in each shop. It didn't take the police long to track them down, but this open-and-shut case rapidly began to burst at the seams when the robbers declared that they had carried out the raids on the orders of their 'queen'. There followed a court case so strange that it has gone down in US legal history.

The queen in question was Queen Shahmia. She used to go under the far more normal name of Richell Denise Clark Bradshaw – until 1991, when she discovered that she was the daughter of God and bride of Christ. Over the next few years after that astounding revelation, she gathered a cluster of devoted followers who treated her with absolute reverence. One of the witnesses at her trial, Ismael Castilleja, explained how he often bowed before Queen Shahmia. He gave her money, he ate on the floor while she ate at a table, and slept on the floor while she slept on a bed. 'We do not do anything without her permission,' he testified.

Her other followers used to bathe her, rub lotion on her feet and peel her fruit. They cooked for her and cleaned for her. It was, said Queen Shahmia, because of the great 'love' they felt towards her. They proved their faith when Shahmia decided she wanted to stay in a luxury hotel and, according to Castilleja's testimony, ordered her servants to go 'plunder the earth' to raise the necessary funds. The results were captured on those in-store security cameras, and when the link was made to Queen Shahmia it was discovered that she was responsible for a mini-crimewave across the state of Florida.

Even after she was captured, Shahmia showed no sign that she planned to renounce her sovereignty. Most of her servants stuck by her too. One, a maid called Nirishi, insisted that she would still wear her necklace made from Shahmia's clipped fingernails and chose to stay by her queen rather than keep custody of her own children.

Shahmia, for her part, denied ever telling anyone to steal. 'God is going to have his way. If prison is where he chooses I go, I go with a beautiful smile,' she told Judge Thomas Reese before sentencing. 'I have not deceived. I have not lied. I am Queen Shahmia.'

Judge Reese gave her 25 years.

Raëlism

Founded: 1973.

Country of origin: France.

Gods and guiding voices: Raël, the Elohim.

Membership: 55,000 claimed worldwide.

Texts: Claude Vorilhon: *The Message Given To Me By Extraterrestrials*; Claude Vorilhon: *Sensual Meditation: Awakening The Mind By Awakening The Body*; Claude Vorilhon: *Space Aliens Took Me To Their Planet*; Claude Vorilhon: *Yes To Human Cloning: Eternal Human Life Thanks To Science*; Claude Vorilhon: *Let's Welcome Our Fathers From Outer Space: They Created Humanity In Their Laboratories*.

Basic beliefs: Humanity was created 25,000 years ago, cloned by alien scientists called the Elohim. We need to set up an embassy for the

Elohim so they can come back to Earth. Meanwhile, let's have some sexy massages.

The advocates of Raëlism are either scientific geniuses or promotional masterminds – and as their prophet and founder Raël has pointed out, they win both ways. In late December 2002 they gained front-page headlines throughout the world when they claimed that researchers in their company Clonaid had created the world's first human clone. This was a baby girl called Eve, whom Clonaid claimed was genetically identical to one of its parents. She was born by Caesarean section on the night after Christmas.

Top scientists quickly derided the claim as a technological impossibility. Clonaid initially promised to allow them to carry out independent tests, but then withdrew the offer, saying that they were concerned about the welfare of Eve and her 'parents' and wanted to protect themselves from prosecution (human cloning is illegal in most countries). The world's press began to dismiss the whole thing as a hoax – but not before Raël and his movement had received millions of dollars' worth of free publicity and ensured human cloning remained where they wanted it on the political agenda – right at the top.

Cloning is a subject dear to Raël's heart. He not only teaches that the process will form the key to human immortality (when technology is advanced far enough to transfer the memory and personality of a person into their genetically identical double) but also that it was the way in which humanity was created in the first place. We were, he

says, cooked up 25,000 years ago as part of a scientific experiment in the laboratories of a race of benevolent space aliens called the Elohim.

Raël first came across the Elohim in 1973 when he still went by the name of Claude Vorilhon and worked as a motoring journalist. According to his book *The Message Given To Me By Extraterrestrials*, Vorilhon was walking in a volcanic mountain range in his native France when he came across a flying object the size of a small bus sporting a cone with a flashing red light on top and hovering several yards above the ground. A four-foot-tall extraterrestrial in a green, one-piece suit, and with almond-shaped eyes, long, black hair, a black beard and slightly greenish skin, stepped out of this spacecraft and told Vorilhon that he had been selected to spread a message of love, peace and fraternity to all humanity. Vorilhon spent the next few days with the little man – who was called Yahweh, just like the creator of humanity in the Bible – and learned all about the history of the Elohim. He also began to understand his own mission to help set up an embassy for these aliens so that they can eventually make their official reappearance on Earth and give us their wisdom and technology.

A couple of years later, when Vorilhon had taken on the name Raël and was already telling the world of his experiences, the Elohim whisked him away for a holiday on their home planet. There, the Elohim piped knowledge directly into his brain and he met several of Earth's other leading prophets, including Jesus, Buddha, Joseph Smith (see **The Latter-day Saints**) and Mohammed. Jesus, said Raël, is a very beautiful man – and very thin.

Later, a robot showed Raël to his room and asked him if he wanted a female companion. Raël, who has something of a reputation as a ladies' man, said '*Oui*'. He was then presented with a beautiful, brunette, biological sex robot. Then a blonde appeared. Then a redhead. Then a 'magnificent' black woman. Then a 'very fine' Chinese lady and then another voluptuous Asian. Raël just couldn't decide which of the 'girls' to test drive. Luckily, the robot said he could take all six and he shared an 'unforgettable' bath with them.

There's good news for humanity, as Raël says that soon we will all be serviced by these endlessly compliant nanobots. He acknowledges that 'feminists' might not like the idea – but then he points out that nobody has any problem about using washing machines or a dishwasher, so why should it be different with sex robots? What's more, he says, all this android action will remove the curse of jealousy from human relations forever.

Even before the robots came along, Raël had plenty of ways of keeping his followers happy. He's a firm believer in freedom within consensual adult relationships, and many adherents have been attracted to his Sensual Meditation seminars where he teaches them how to awaken the potential of their bodies for pleasure and love, how to get in touch with their erogenous zones, and how to inspect their bottoms using a mirror.

Until Clonaid was set up in the late 1990s, it was these erotic aspects of Raël's movement that caused the most controversy. Critics claimed that lonely men were attracted to the group in the hope of getting some orgy action. Raël meanwhile (or 'His Holiness' as he preferred to be called), in contradiction to his liberationist philosophy, was said to have told many of his most attractive female followers that they must preserve their sexual favours for the unique enjoyment of the prophets. Of course, this would have redounded to Raël's advantage, as there's only one prophet around at the moment – him.

In spite of these criticisms, the group has so far been mercifully free of any of the accusations of paedophilia and physical or mental abuse that plague other similar groups. Anti-cult activists have now focused their attention on the apparent scam relating to human cloning. The Raëlists, for their part, claim to have produced another twelve cloned babies since Eve and say that thanks to all the publicity they've been getting, their membership has risen to around the 65,000 mark and their beliefs have spread to more than 80 countries. Because of the secrecy that now surrounds their cloning operations, these assertions are no more – or less – verifiable than Raël's declarations about his frequent contacts with the Elohim.

A Silly Old Cult!
The Ranters
Founded: 1649.
Country of origin: England.

There were so many strange sects and extreme movements knocking around in the turbulent years following the English Civil War that many hardly even registered at the time – and many more have been forgotten since. There was no ignoring the Ranters, however. If we are to believe the many detractors that wrote about them, their behaviour

was extreme even by the mad standards of the day. Declaring that sin is just an illusion and that no action is immoral if done in a spirit of purity, they engaged in wife-swapping, public sex, drunkenness, swearing and theft with enthusiastic abandon (see picture: The Ranters Ranting). To cement their reputation, they communed in alehouses and only went to a regular pews-and-altar church if they wanted to shout abuse at the vicar.

Of course, few things annoyed the puritans in Cromwell's England more than people cavorting in their birthday suits and having guilt-free fun. The Ranters were ruthlessly put down. In 1650 many were rounded up under special new laws against blasphemy, and forced to recant. Even so, they managed to remain active in some areas up until the restoration of Charles II in 1660 and a few lasted for decades more on Long Island and other similarly untamed parts of the American colonies. Those were the days.

Roman Catholicism

Founded: AD 325.
Country of origin: Judea.
Gods and guiding voices: 'God', Jesus Christ, St Augustine.
Membership: One billion.
Texts: The Bible.
Basic beliefs: Jesus is the son of God. The Pope is infallible. Every sperm is sacred. Wine turns to blood when you drink it!

The Roman Catholic Church is responsible, directly or indirectly, for more murders than any other organisation in history. From the witch-hunts of the fourth century up until their support of fascism and denial of contraception to Africa in the twentieth century, the Papacy has a record of killing that makes US governments look like upstart amateurs by comparison. It's ironic, given their uncompromising stance on abortion and contraception, but Catholicism has been a highly effective check on world population growth. (See Appendix 4 for more details.)

The Church is also the oldest continually operating institution in existence – and they've had to be tough to stay pre-eminent for so long. The fact that they managed to survive the first few hundred years of their existence, for instance, is incredible enough. It wasn't just the vague sporadic persecutions of the Roman Empire that they had to contend with – their whole theological system was a confusing mess. Up until the middle of the second century there had been no attempt to create anything like a coherent testament of their leader Jesus

Christ. There were upwards of thirty contradictory gospels kicking around (not to mention all the other stories relating to dozens of other remarkably similar Messiah figures from the same era). What's more, in spite of all this diversity, many early communities didn't have a single book between them. It was a miracle of organisation to arrive at a consensus relating to the gospels of Matthew, Mark, Luke and John – and these in turn were miraculous books; seemingly written after their supposed authors (who, judging by their position in ancient society, should probably have been illiterate) had died. It's also rather wonderful that the books were composed in Greek rather than the writers' native Aramaic.

Even when the early Christians had some semblance of a Bible, they didn't know what to believe. There were all kinds of confusing issues. There was the fact that the benevolent God was supposed to have created the entire universe, but according to the gospels it was peopled by demons. Then there was the confusion surrounding the issue of God laying down strict rules, but forgiving sinners (if so, why not sin anyway?). Also, there was the problem of Jesus. Where was he for a start? Hadn't he promised to come back – and bring about the end of the world – shortly after the destruction of the temple in Jerusalem, which occurred in AD 70? Why did the divine Jesus suffer at his death? How was he born of a nonphysical God? Or was he in fact a God who wasn't born at all?

This last question proved to be the most vexing during the period after the Emperor Constantine converted to Christianity in 312. It was partly to solve it that the Council of Nicaea was held in 325 and the first Catholic Church institution was created. The Council decided (relying on a vote rather than divine inspiration) that Jesus was not a created being. Then, instituting a long and effective Roman Catholic tradition, Constantine ordered that all books suggesting Christ was a created being should be burned and he exiled the theory's leading proponent, Arius. The emperor also helped create a hierarchical system for the Church and told the bishops to wear expensive robes. Meanwhile, some of the greatest geniuses of the age like St Jerome and St Augustine set to explaining the apparent contradictions and reams of nonsense in the Bible – and, in the case of Augustine, ensuring that anyone who didn't agree with them was tortured.

Catholicism was on its way to becoming the single biggest faith group known to man. In spite of a few blips like the reign of Julian the Apostate (a Roman Emperor who worshipped the old Olympian gods) the Catholic Church went from strength to strength. Less than a hundred years after Nicaea it was pre-eminent. There were still plenty of old-fashioned pagans around, but a few bloody witch-hunts and increasingly hardline persecution from the end of the fourth century ensured that they generally kept quiet.

As the Roman Empire changed shape so much that it became unrecognisable, the Church remained constant. It was one of the few institutions in the West wealthy and powerful enough to maintain libraries and scholarship through the Dark Ages. This stranglehold on learning enabled the Church to influence which versions of history people would be able to read for generations to come, by the selection of some books for preservation and the destruction of others.

Even while it was so dominant in the Dark Ages, the Catholic Church had to face off a few unpleasant facts. For instance, some time around the tenth century, scholars began to agree that the world was round rather than flat (as the Bible presumed). Then the Eastern Orthodox Church split from Rome in the Great Schism of the eleventh century. However, it wasn't until the advent of the printing press that things began to get really tricky again. The worst setbacks occurred when the Bible was translated into languages other than Latin and distributed widely enough so that people actually began to read what it said. The resultant mess of ideas saw almost half of Europe split from the Catholic Church, goaded on by fiery preachers like the permanently constipated Martin Luther and fun-hating Calvin. Luckily, for the faith, the Vatican was able to maintain its wealth levels with South American gold – and it spread into as many territories as it seemed to have lost (even though that did involve wiping out most of

the previous inhabitants in one of the most effective genocides humanity has ever seen. Whether or not the European conquerors deliberately aided the spread of the smallpox which decimated the Indian population is a matter of debate (although by the time they got

Cult Hero

SIMEON OF STYLITES

Simeon of Stylites made his name by standing on a pillar (*style* is the Greek word for pillar). He stood there, overlooking the mountain ridge of Telnesin in Syria, for more than thirty years, sixty-feet high in the air, his feet fastened to the stone of the column.

An average day would find him up before dawn, arms and eyes raised to heaven in prayer. He only changed position when he wanted to bow. His (anonymous) biographer declared that 'the joints of his vertebrae were dislocated from continuous supplication'.

At around 9 a.m., crowds began to gather and he started to preach and get stuck into some serious denouncing – his preferred targets being pagans, heretics and Jews.

In the afternoons, pilgrims (once even including the Roman Emperor Theodoric) would climb a ladder up the side of Simeon's column to take his counsel. Or at least, they'd climb halfway up the ladder. Accounts declare that his smell was so overpowering few people could get closer to him. The foul odour was largely attributed to his left foot, which was full of ulcers and, apparently, alive with maggots.

Once a week, Simeon ate some food – except during Lent, when he tried not to eat at all.

At night, like many half-starved ascetics, he hallucinated and imagined he was fighting the devil.

On the morning of 2 September 459 he was found dead, clinging to the edge of his pillar. He'd been there for 36 years.

He has been revered as a Saint ever since.

to the mainland they were fully aware of the effects of the disease on Indian populations, having seen it devastate the native populations of Cuba and Hispanola). However, there's no doubting the intent of the production-line system that priests developed for baptising Indian babies before bashing their brains out on rocks – claiming they were doing them a favour by sending them straight to heaven.

The Renaissance caused yet more problems when lippy brainboxes like Galileo started contradicting the Church's belief that the Earth was the centre of the universe, and came up with all kinds of troublesome proofs that wouldn't go away even after the traditional application of torture and a few judicious executions.

Still, the Church survived almost intact, and since those turbulent years the Papacy has managed to keep things on a relatively even keel. It's successfully weathered the scientific and historical battering the Bible has taken since the age of Enlightenment and, in fact, this ancient edifice has settled surprisingly comfortably into the modern world. It even managed to escape answering too many uncomfortable questions after the priesthood helped Franco achieve power in Spain, tacitly supported Mussolini in Italy and said virtually nothing against Hitler in Germany – until it was too late.

Nowadays, the Roman Catholic hierarchy is facing persistent criticism about the child abuse carried out by many of its priests – and its failure to address the issue. Many churches have even been accused of actively trying to conceal the crimes. in 2005 there was also the uncomfortable (for some) spectacle of the supposedly infallible Pope John Paul II dying slowly in front of the world's cameras, unable to speak at many of his last public functions and clearly in terrible pain. He was replaced by the man formerly known as the 'bad cop' of the church hierarchy, Benedict XVI (AKA 'The Enforcer', AKA 'God's Rottweiler', AKA 'The Grand Inquisitor'). Pope Benedict is a reactionary who has described other religions as 'deficient', sees homosexuality as intrinsically evil, denounced rock music as 'the vehicle of anti-religion' and, tragically, insists that the use of contraception – AIDS or no AIDS – is a sin. Aged 78, he was backed up by all the wealth and power of the Roman Catholic Church and the combined faith of its one billion members. It seems like an awful long way from those obscure events in Judea.

The Church of Satan, AKA Satanism.

Founded: 1966.

Country of Origin: USA.

Gods and guiding voices: The individual.

Membership: Figures not available.

Famous associates past and present: Jayne Mansfield, Sammy Davis Jnr, Marilyn Manson.

Basic beliefs: The individual is master of his own destiny. Conventional religions are full of bunk. What theologians regard as man's predilection for evil will always outweigh the good. So – from the theological point of view – we are evil individuals. Evil is just 'live' written backwards and should be enjoyed.

Words of Wisdom

' Satan has been the best friend the church has ever had, as he has kept it in business all these years! **'**

Anton LaVey

HOLY SMOKE!

THE SATANIC PANIC (I)

During the 1980s alarming stories began to spread out from right-wing evangelical Christian circles. Organised and secretive Satan-worshipping groups were wreaking havoc across the free world. There were reports of ritual sacrifice, cannibalism, Black Masses, mock marriages, people being kept naked in snake-filled cages or buried alive, forced demonic pregnancies, murder (estimates

Don't be confused by the name. Members of the Church of Satan don't actually worship the bad guy with cloven hooves and a pitchfork. For them, Satan personifies an ethos rather than actually being the famous person from the Bible. He represents the adversary of all man-made spiritual religions and the personification of life.

The always amusing founder of the Church, Anton LaVey, said he codified Satanism after first toying with the idea of Dogism. Dogism holds that 'if you can't eat it or fuck it, piss on it'. Satanism is far more complex. LaVey laid out the groundwork for the belief system in the international bestseller *The Satanic Bible*. He said that the Christian church and most other religions are outdated and hypocritical. They are 'contemptible crutches', which man has invented to help him come to terms with his own mortality and fallibility. What's more, most religions are centred on denying basic human nature, and what they call 'sins' are actually fundamental human needs, essential for living a happy life.

LaVey used the Seven Deadly Sins as an example. He said that greed, pride, envy, anger, sloth, gluttony and lust are all essential to living a happy and fulfilling life. Lust, for one, not only leads to love, but without it there would be no families and no continuation of the race. Anyone wearing an article of clothing not essential for protection from the elements is guilty of pride – which covers just about everyone not from a Third World country. Being reluctant to get out of bed in the morning is sloth – which again means that just about everyone is therefore culpable. And so it goes on. Anger is

vital for self-preservation. Gluttony is eating more than you need to live. Greed is wanting more than you already have. Envy is liking the possessions of others and wanting the same for yourself. These so-called 'sins' are actually the basic components of ambition – and without ambition little would ever have been accomplished in the world.

There was more to LaVey than just diabolically clever philosophy. Before he shaved his head (executioner-style) and declared that it was the Year Zero *Anno Satinis* (1966 to you and me), LaVey had had a rich and varied career as a carnival follower, a big-top calliope (steam organ) player and magician's assistant. He was consequently able to

went up to 10,000 a year and higher) and narcolepsy. Some even ranted about babies cooked in microwaves and sacrifices carried out in the bowels of the UK House of Commons.

The most troubling and persistent rumours of satanic ritual abuse concerned the molestation of minors. They started when Lawrence Pazder's book *Michelle Remembers* became a transatlantic bestseller. It was published as fact – but soon investigators were labelling it a hoax. Not soon enough to stop the witch-hunt, however, and dozens of people were thrown in jail. Nearly all the convictions were eventually overturned when the lurid accusations were attributed to false memory syndrome. (The courts concluded that there was no real evidence other than the testimony of children influenced by manipulative questioning, usually from Christian therapists.) In the early 1990s, a University of California study investigating more

183

than 12,000 accusations and interviewing 11,000 psychiatric, social service, and law enforcement personnel came to the conclusion that there was no unequivocal evidence for a single case of satanic abuse.

THE SATANIC PANIC (II)

Over recent years satanic ritual abuse has become a self-fulfilling prophecy (one of the few prophecies to come out of the evangelical community that's been fulfilled). Large groups of 1980s children, brought up on all those vivid stories of the evils of Satan, have developed a worrying taste for black make-up, ear-splitting death metal and killing each other in weird rites. On 22 February 2005 for instance, Andrea Volpe (now in his twenties), the leader of the Italian rock band Beasts Of Satan, was sentenced to thirty years in prison for killing the group's singer and two women in 'Satanic' ritual murders. A few months before in Edinburgh, Luke Mitchell, a

bring great showbiz pizzazz to his role as Devil's Advocate. Few journalists met the 'massive', 'dark' and 'intelligent' man without feeling impressed, while the house he lived in (painted completely black on the outside) was a constant source of amusement thanks to its rooms hidden behind mummy cases, secret panels and the presence of a basement Ritual Chamber, complete with Hammond Organ.

The Church grew slowly at first and LaVey held kitsch nightclub rituals featuring bikini-clad vixens to raise money. For a while he also took on the part of an impish agony aunt by running a weekly tabloid column, 'Letters from the Devil'. Among other things, he told interested readers how to brew their own love potions and make their own voodoo dolls. Luckily for him, his unique combination of occultism, bikinis and church-baiting rhetoric gradually caught on. Although LaVey was forever expressing his exasperation at the 'losers' who tried to join his church expecting kinky sex and orgies, the fact that naked women serve as altars during Church of Satan rites probably gained them a few members. When LaVey landed the part of Old Scratch himself in Roman Polanski's hit horror film *Rosemary's Baby* he was catapulted to international notoriety. The Church has maintained steady numbers since then (it's hard to know exactly how many practising members there are as they keep the identities secret, mainly, they claim, for the individuals' protection from overzealous Christian neighbours), but since the death of the charismatic LaVey in 1997 doubt has been cast on the organisation's long-term survival. Nevertheless, his spiritual descendants insist that they're going to carry on doing the devil's work.

sixteen-year-old obsessed with Satan, knives and the number 666, was found guilty of murdering his girlfriend. Meanwhile the satanic Norwegian 'Black metal' community has been decimated by ritual killings and the Roman Catholic Church is promising to stoke the hellfire further by bringing back exorcism.

Sathya Sai Baba

Founded: 1925.
Country of origin: India.
Gods and guiding voices: Sathya Sai Baba.
Membership: Estimates vary between 1 million and 16 million
Famous associates: Isaac Tigrett, co-founder of the Hard Rock Café chain.
Texts: Sathya Sai Baba: *Sathya Sai Speaks (volumes 1–34)*; Dr John S Hislop: *Sai Baba – The Man of Miracles.*
Basic beliefs: Sathya Sai Baba is an avatar, a living incarnation of a god. He can do magic!

Sathya Sai Baba is one of the world's most successful gurus. He has millions of followers and the wealth to match. He claims to be omniscient, omnipotent and omnipresent; and who's to doubt him when (unlike Jesus, as he's fond of pointing out) he's around to perform miracles in front of his followers' very eyes. He's said to be able to cure the sick and resuscitate the dead. He's multiplied food and turned water into petrol. From his mouth he can produce five-inch lingams (lingams are stone penises, Hindu fertility symbols). From thin air he has been seen to pluck pendants, chains, rings, necklaces and photographs. From his bare palms he has scattered ash on the ground.

If any more proof of the old sage's power were needed it came on his seventieth birthday when more than a million people, including the president and prime minister of India, assembled around his ashram in Prasanthi Nilayam to pay homage to him. He's also extremely popular with rich Europeans and Americans. Isaac Tigrett, who co-founded the Hard Rock Café chain, took Sai Baba's phrase – 'Love All, Serve All' – and made it the motto of the famous eateries. Tigrett also helped fund a massive hospital and clean water project near Sai Baba's home in India, earning the guru the undying love of thousands of poor followers.

It seems surprising therefore, that in the face of all this power and munificence many cynics have denounced Sai Baba as a fake. One man, Basava Premanand, devoted thirty years of his life to exposing what he sees as Baba's lies and exploitation. He even taught himself all of Baba's 'magic' tricks – right down to the dramatic swallowing of glass – and dismissed them as nothing more than advanced conjuring. In 2004 the BBC TV programme 'The Secret Swami' further damaged the Afro-haired holy man by capturing his sleights of hand on camera. His miracles, it seemed, were no more impressive than David Blaine's. In fact, as one reviewer pointed out, on that basis we'd be as well off worshipping Blaine as Baba.

Less amusingly, the BBC programme reinstated the rumours of sexual abuse that have plagued the Sai Baba camp for the past thirty years. Several teenagers were interviewed who claimed to have been molested by the old man. They related terrible stories of the guru's requests for them to oil his privates and inspect them with their tongues. As one scholar pointed out, this is not a practice sanctioned by Hindu scripture or tradition. Worship of the lingam does not extend to blow jobs.

Recently the US embassy has also posted a warning about the holy man's alleged sexual activities and UNESCO has withdrawn from a conference with his organisation because of their concerns about the allegations. No official investigation has been undertaken to date, although even that probably wouldn't make too much difference to his devoted followers. Isaac Tigrett, for instance, declared that the guru could go out and murder someone and that wouldn't change his 'evolution'.

Meanwhile the eighty-something Sai Baba is still going strong, and claims he will continue to do so until the age of 96, when he will depart this life. It will be interesting to see if he's as good at predicting the future as he is at conjuring Rolexes from the air.

Scientology

Founded: 1954.

Country of origin: USA.

Gods and guiding voices: All and any – the church claims that it's possible to be a Scientologist and still hold other faiths.

Membership: They say millions. Even detractors say there are at least 500,000.

Famous associates (past and present): Tom Cruise, John Travolta, Kirstie Alley, Beck, Lisa-Marie Presley, Juliette Lewis, Patrick Swayze, Chick Corea and Nancy Cartwright (the voice of Bart Simpson).

Texts: L Ron Hubbard: *Dianetics: The Modern Science Of Mental Health*; L Ron Hubbard: *Scientology: The Fundamentals Of Thought*; L Ron Hubbard: *What Is Scientology?*

Basic beliefs: Man is a spiritual being – and immortal. He has unlimited capabilities and experience that stretches way beyond a single lifetime. These capabilities are held in check by 'the reactive mind'. This can be dealt with using techniques and disciplines available through the Church. Apparently, a naughty alien called Xenu caused a lot of trouble on Earth 75 million years ago – trouble which has startling repercussions today.

The fastest-growing religion on Earth (according to their own website at least) had its origins in 1950s America when pulp sci-fi author L Ron Hubbard published a book called *Dianetics.*

Dianetics was a guide to a therapeutic technique, which the author claimed could cure all mental illnesses and psychosomatic illnesses (illnesses caused by the mind). Since Hubbard claimed that nearly seventy per cent of seemingly physical illnesses were actually caused

HOLY SMOKE!

WORD UP

Hubbard's was a highly creative mind. He came up with more neologisms than most authors since the time of Shakespeare. The most important are related to the system of Dianetics counselling in which a series of tests known as 'auditing', or 'clearing' are used to help eliminate the 'reactive mind' – the mind weakened by harmful experiences. These experiences are engraved in mental pictures called 'engrams', many of which have happened in the past lives of the subject's true self. The true self is known as the 'thetan'.

by the mind, this was a fair old whack of man's ills. Hubbard had struck gold. Although it's easy to mock its pseudo-scientific approach, contradictions and poorly researched claims, there's no denying the originality of Dianetics. It was one of the first great self-help guides of the twentieth century and it sold by the truckload.

Not all of the medical profession was convinced, however. A leading psychoanalyst at the time, Rollo May, voiced the sentiments of many when he wrote in the *New York Times*: 'Books like this do harm by their grandiose promises to troubled persons and by their oversimplification of human psychological problems.'

So, Hubbard's attempts to practise his therapy soon attracted the unwelcome attention of concerned medical practitioners. His increasing fortune also became more and more interesting to the US tax authorities. These problems were solved when Hubbard established the religion that he was to head (spiritually at least, although he formally relinquished control in the 1970s) until the end of his life. As luck would have it, Hubbard could now claim that his Dianetics procedures were a part of the Church's sacred liturgy rather than 'medical'. What's more, religions are exempt from paying tax in the USA.

By the 1960s Hubbard was claiming that ever-higher levels of spiritual enlightenment could be obtained by repeated testing and spiritual auditing. Members of the Church could gradually climb the scale until they received godlike powers of awareness, freedom from disease and mental control. This progression didn't come cheap,

however. It still doesn't. Some estimates have put the cost to an average person of getting to the top of the ladder of Scientology at up to $500,000.

This high cost of being a Scientologist has been one of the most consistent criticisms levelled at the Church over the years. There have also been repeated accusations of psychological damage inflicted on people involved with the group (several of whom have successfully sued, and won thousands of dollars). These issues were highlighted in an excoriating article for *Time* magazine in 1991: 'The Thriving Cult Of Greed And Power'. Millions of readers around the world must have been interested to read that eleven high-ranking members of the church, including Hubbard's wife, had been arrested in the 1980s for

Scientologists had long described CAN as a 'hate group' and even picketed meetings that Kisser was attending, but things didn't really start to heat up until shortly after the 1991 'Cult Of Greed' *Time* magazine article. This piece claimed that the Cult Awareness Network received more calls for help about Scientology than any of the other 200 'mind control' organisations that it monitored and Kisser was quoted as saying that Scientology was quite likely to be the 'most ruthless' cult in American history.

Not long afterwards, CAN was bombarded by applications from Scientologists wanting to join up. When Kisser refused them, the writs started pouring in. CAN was hit by more than fifty lawsuits (twelve arriving in one week according to Kisser) declaring that she was discriminating against the Scientologist applicants. Most of the cases were eventually dropped or won

'infiltrating, burglarising and wiretapping' upwards of a hundred private and government agencies, and about the 'Mafia'-like activities of the Scientologists.

The writer Richard Behar also detailed a policy Hubbard had instituted known as 'Fair Game', according to which all perceived enemies of Scientology were subject to being 'tricked, sued or lied to, or destroyed'. Those who criticise the Church, said Behar, often found themselves engulfed in litigation, stalked by private detectives, beaten up or even threatened with death. The Scientologists responded to the attack with typical subtlety: they launched a multimillion-dollar lawsuit against *Time* magazine. Five years after the article was published, the US Supreme Court threw out all the claims against the magazine. Meanwhile, Behar was moved to file his own counterclaim, alleging that the Scientologists used private investigators to harass him, illegally obtained copies of his credit report and telephone records, and contacted his friends and neighbours to ask about his health, whether he had tax problems and even whether he had ever taken drugs.

Since then, thanks to the advent of the Internet, ever more fascinating aspects of the Scientology system have become common knowledge. The story that's really tickled the Church's detractors relates to a series of documents first published in the *Los Angeles Times* (who accessed them during a court case that the Church of Scientology was involved in). These were written in Hubbard's own handwriting and detailed where the harmful 'engrams' in the world come from. This information, claim the Internerds, is given to Scientologists when they reach the advanced level of clearing known as OT III – (generally after about five years and $50,000). Hubbard used to claim that the knowledge gained at this level was powerful enough to kill anyone not prepared for it.

The gist of this fascinating story is that mankind's problems began 75 million years ago when the planet Earth (then called Teegeeach) was part of a confederation of ninety planets under the leadership of a tyrannical ruler named Xenu. Xenu cured intergalactic overpopulation by paralysing the people of the other planets, flying them to Earth in space planes, plopping them down near volcanoes and dropping H-bombs on them. The souls of these murdered people (more accurately the 'thetans') were then taken to cinemas and shown films for several days. The end result was that the souls clustered together and now inhabit people in their thousands. And, of course, they must be removed – at huge expense.

Important Scientologists have denied in the past that this is the literal basis of their religion. But it does help explain where all those pictures of volcanoes on the covers of Hubbard's books come from …

by CAN – but eventually they ended up owing nearly $2million.

The crippling blow came when a Scientology lawyer, Kendrick Moxon, success-fully sued CAN on behalf of his client Jason Scott (then an eighteen-year-old mem-ber of a fringe Pentecostal church, who had been kid-napped by a deprogrammer the Scientologists alleged had been referred to Scott's mother by a volunteer at CAN). In spite of CAN's insistence that it had noth-ing to do with illegal depro-gramming, Scott was awarded $1.8million from the group and it soon went bust.

During the bankruptcy hear-ing, another Scientologist, Steven Hayes, outbid Kisser to the rights to her organi-sation's name. Now the website of the Cult Awareness Network con-tains an article that labels other groups as cults and people who've called the

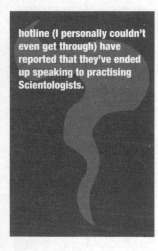

hotline (I personally couldn't even get through) have reported that they've ended up speaking to practising Scientologists.

Cult Hero

L RON HUBBARD

The founder of the Church of Scientology, whose genial old face still beams down from the walls of nearly all Scientology buildings, was by any standard a remarkable man. His written output alone (both as a writer of science fiction, his other speciality, and religious texts) comes to more than seven million words, and his influence on modern humanity is incalculable.

'I have high hopes of smashing my name into history so violently that it will take a legendary form ... That goal is the real goal as far as I am concerned,' he said, writing to the first of his three wives in 1938, more than a decade before he created Scientology. He also told many people that he believed that the best way to make a fortune was to become the founder of a religion. He succeeded beyond any reasonable expectation.

Before he did, however, he tried out black magic. He became deeply involved with the teachings of Aleister Crowley and his disciple Jack Parsons. Hubbard and Parsons practised sex magic and other extreme rites together, but the relationship soured when Hubbard ran off with a quantity of Parsons's money and his girlfriend, Sara Northrup. He then married Northrup before he divorced his first wife.

Hubbard's son, Ron Hubbard Jnr, once told *Penthouse* magazine that during the same post-war period he saw his father carrying out an abortion on his first wife with a coat hanger. He also said that his father believed he was the

Antichrist. Hubbard Jnr compared his father to Hitler. Curiously, considering Scientology's present-day hardline anti-drugs stance, Hubbard Jnr also revealed that his father tried cocaine, amphetamine, peyote and barbiturates. In fact, he said, it would be shorter to list the drugs that the elder Hubbard didn't take.

Many critics still contend that once Hubbard founded Scientology, he ran it on black-magic principles and that there are marked similarities in many of his writings to Aleister Crowley's. Hubbard became far more respectable than his old guru, however, once the cash started flowing in. He even took to insisting that people referred to him as Dr Hubbard. Like that other great American, Hunter S Thompson, he'd invested in a mail-order degree. Unlike 'Doktor' Thompson, Hubbard didn't see this as a joke.

Even at the height of his fame and power Hubbard always kept a suitcase of money with him so he would be able to do a runner whenever circumstances required. Towards the end of his life, it appeared that the suitcase would be urgently needed. High-level defectors from the church began accusing Hubbard of having stolen millions of dollars from its coffers. The American revenue service began seeking an indictment for tax fraud. Hubbard (who had been in hiding for five years) died before the criminal case could be prosecuted – although not before a California judge declared (in a 1984 case in which the Scientologists sued a biographical researcher) that the old man was 'a pathological liar'.

HOLY SMOKE!

A GREAT BIG NARCONON

In February 2005, the State Superintendent urged all schools in California to stop allowing representatives from the Scientology anti-drugs programme Narconon into their classrooms. The *San Francisco Chronicle* had reported that as well as teaching the dangers of drugs, the Narconon men and women had been preaching the benefits of Scientology. Teachers also said that the children were being passed some very suspect information – like the idea that drug residues can be sweated out in saunas and that coloured ooze is produced when drugs exit the body.

ROVING REPORT

One afternoon I decided to take the 'Stress Test' advertised outside the Scientology building on Tottenham Court Road in London. Inside everything seemed cheery. 'Under the Boardwalk' was being piped out of a small stereo and a healthy number of people were drinking tea and chatting.

A pretty girl sat me down next to a box covered in dials and numbers. She handed me two metal tubes, which were attached to the main instrument by two thin wires. She told me to hold one tube in each hand and relax while she asked me a series of questions about my life. I noticed that if I squeezed the tubes, a needle on the machine would zip up on its scale. I squeezed them when she asked about tax. From that, she was able to conclude that I was stressed about my tax bill.

When I asked the girl how the machine worked she just said it was 'special'. I later learned that it was an electropsychometer, a device developed by Scientology engineers in the 1950s. An E-meter, as they're also known, measures changes in electrical resistance in the body. Since a 1960s' US Food and Drug Administration edict, Scientology can no longer refer to E-meters as having any medical use: they are now 'religious artefacts'. The latest Mark VII Quantum, the device I was using, looked like a prop from *Doctor Who*, but celebrities like disco-dancing John Travolta swear by them. You'll have to stump up upwards of

£2,000 if you want to buy one of your own though.

After being shown a film about a young sporting hero, who recovered from a seemingly crippling injury and escaped from a crew of evil psychotherapists – with the help of nothing more than the Dianetics book – I was advised to take a personality test. I answered 200 very personal multiple-choice questions and another woman fed the answers into a computer, frowning over the graph it produced.

'You need help,' she told me. She suggested that maybe a Scientology-approved course in Dianetics would do the trick.

But I couldn't agree with the findings. The graph suggested I had no friends! Soon we were arguing.

'They're your answers, not mine,' she said eventually.

'They're your questions, though, and ...'

'Well then, Mr Sceptic, I can't believe that there's really nothing that you'd like to change about your life.'

'Well, I'd quite like a better haircut,' I said weakly, not wanting to go into such personal matters with a complete stranger.

I began to realise that I wasn't quite as welcome as I had been. Earlier on, my questioner had been full of smiles and given to long hard looks into my eyes and slightly over-lingering bodily contact. Now she was grimacing and barely holding back from shouting.

I had to get the big question in before I was asked to leave.

'To be honest, this isn't quite what I was expecting,' I said.

'How do you mean?'

'Well, I was told that there's lots of stuff about aliens.'

She pushed her chair back and leaped to her feet. 'What a load of crap!' she yelled, visibly shaken and starting to splutter. 'Do you …? Where did you hear about that?'

'Er –'

'Come on! It's bullshit. Do I look like the kind of person that would believe in aliens?'

'Er,' I was floundering too. 'Maybe I read it in relation to Tom Cruise or something. Something about –'

'Oh please. Tom Cruise is one of the nicest people I've ever met. Does he look like the kind of person that you'd find dancing around with aliens?'

It was a question I honestly couldn't answer.

I wondered if I should ask about Xenu but the woman was already standing up. She shot me one last withering look.

'You,' she hissed, 'need to take a good look at your reactive mind!'

I got my coat and left.

A Silly Old Cult!

The Society of Women in the Wilderness

Founded: 1693.

Country of origin: Germany.

Gods and guiding voices: 'God'.

Membership: 40.

Basic beliefs: The world was due to end in 1694; 40 is a good number.

German prophet Johann Jacob Zimmerman decided that The End was due to come in 1694 and that the big moment's ground zero was located in the untamed wilds of America. On the shores of the Wissahickon river in Pennsylvania, to be exact.

Before Zimmerman could lead his followers to the Promised Land, he died. Luckily, they soon found a new leader in Johannes Kelpius, a numerologist obsessed with the number 40. He led a group of German followers to the wilds of Pennsylvania in the USA, convinced that God would reveal himself in the nature there. The group was made up entirely of men so, naturally enough, it soon became known as 'The Society of Women in the Wilderness'. These men (not coincidentally, there were forty of them) built a 40-foot-square tabernacle and then settled down in their 40-foot-square cabin to wait for the end of time, peering out through a primitive telescope set on their communal cabin's rooftop, anxious not to be caught off guard when the Rapture began.

The year 1694 passed peacefully enough, but Kelpius reset the big date and the monks stayed on, playing music and growing vegetables together until Kelpius died in 1708 – not long before his 40th birthday.

A Silly Old Cult!

The Thugs, AKA the Thuggees, AKA the Phansigars.
Founded: Some time in the thirteenth century.
Country of origin: India.
Gods and guiding voices: Kali.
Membership: Figures not available.
Basic beliefs: Murder is a sacred rite in the worship of the goddess of destruction Kali.

When the British annexed India in the late eighteenth century, they were surprised to note that the roads of the country seemed to be swarming with robbers – and that these robbers invariably strangled their victims. They only realised what was going on when Robert

Sherwood, a doctor working in Madras, managed to talk to some of the throttle-happy bandits. They told him that they committed the murders as a religious duty in worship of the dark mother Kali (a female aspect of the Hindu godhead representing destruction and creation).

This strange group were known as the Thugs, a word that rapidly became part of the English language when Sherwood published his sensational findings. In an article, entitled 'On the murderers called Phansigars' (Phansigar was the other nickname for the Thugs; it means noose-operators), Sherwood described the methods of the bandits in great detail. Surprisingly, he said, the Thugs lived quietly in their homes for most of the year, living normal lives and arousing no suspicion. Even their wives were generally ignorant about their double lives as members of a murderous cult. Induction was passed down secretly from father to son.

In the month of pilgrimage, they gathered together in gangs of 10 to 200 men and travelled throughout the country, always taking care to be more than 100 miles from their own native villages. On the roads, an advance party would approach groups of wealthy-looking travellers and ask if they could walk along with them, since there was safety in numbers. A few days later, more Thugs would ask to join them. A few days later, more still. This would continue until there were more Thugs than there were wayfarers. The Thugs would then entertain and cook for their fellow travellers to get them off their guard. They would strike when a favourable opportunity arose –

generally when the travellers were sitting around the fire. A signal was given (often the phrase 'bring the tobacco') and a Thug would place a handkerchief or noose around the victim's neck and start throttling. Another would grab the legs of the poor unfortunate and lift him clear off the ground, while a third grabbed his hands or knelt on his back. The murders didn't last much longer than a few seconds.

After the entire travelling party had been killed, the cultists hacked up the bodies (to make them harder to identify) and buried them. The *Kussee* – a special pickaxe – was placed near the grave, the leader of the group prayed to Kali for wealth and success, a symbolic strangling was enacted and then all those who had played an active role in the murders ate special communion sugar. A (significant) portion of the spoils was set aside for the goddess and then the Thugs went on their way.

It's been estimated that anything up to two million people died at the hands of the Thugs over the centuries, but little systematic effort was made to stop them before the British arrived. Assassination for gain was a religious duty and they considered it a holy and honourable profession, in which moral feelings did not come into play. Some Thugs even paid taxes on their spoils to their local rulers (who themselves weren't that bothered about their activities as long as they took place far from their own lands).

By the beginning of the nineteenth century, Thugs were killing upwards of 40,000 people a year but, even after they began the attempt to wipe them out, the British had to confess a grudging admiration for them. The assistant of William Sleeman, the man eventually assigned to wipe out the Thugs, described a Thug chief as 'the best man I have ever known', while Sir William's grandson compared another to the celebrated dandy Beau Nash. One colonial family were amazed when the man who had been looking after their children and went away for a month each year to see his 'sick mother' was arrested as a Thug. For the rest of the time, he was, like most of his other pious brethren, a model subject.

Even when the repression of the Thugs hit full spate it was always remarked how bravely they met their deaths. Even so, by 1850 more than 4,000 had been arrested. Combined with the improved road system that developed in nineteenth-century India, this ensured that the religion of the Thugs eventually became a thing of the past. Although, of course, the word remains.

A Silly Old Cult!
The Ticklers
Founded: Not known.
Country of origin: Russia.

These were a group of nineteenth-century Russians who believed that the way to religious ecstasy lay in tickling each other. The most extreme Ticklers sometimes managed to work themselves to a state of exhaustion and even death: the latter was considered especially lucky as it guaranteed eternal salvation. Sadly, little else is known about this wonderfully eccentric sect.

Truth Missionaries Chapter of Positive Accord
Founded: 1973.
Country of origin: USA.
Gods and guiding voices: 'God' (Ms).
Membership: Figures not available.
Texts: The Bible.
Basic beliefs: God is doing it.

In contradiction of all those gloomy Nietzschean philosophers who claim that God is dead, as well as those too-clever-by-half atheists who've worked out that He doesn't exist, the Truth Missionaries Chapter of Positive Accord believe that God is alive and well. What's more, She (yes, She's female) is getting it on up in heaven – and enjoying it too.

Most Christian fundamentalists use the Bible to prove that God frowns on people having sex for fun, but the Truth Missionaries Chapter of Positive Accord (TMC+A for short) believe that that's just what She's doing. Both Yahweh and Jesus are this all-powerful, all-horny Goddess's consorts. She is, in fact, their 'Divine Mistress'.

Strangely, the group has remained small. That's in spite of their upbeat philosophy and vaguely kinky beliefs and the US-wide newspaper adverts they've published about their beliefs ('NONE of them has ever been refuted'). Recently, in fact, hardly anything has been heard from them at all. Perhaps, like God, they've diverted their attention to more important matters.

Unarius

Founded: 1954.
Country of origin: USA.
Gods and guiding voices: The Pleiadeans.
Membership: Although Unarius say they have 500,000 students worldwide, some journalists have claimed they have less than 1,000.
Texts: Ernest Norman: *Voice Of Venus*; Charles Spiegel: *The Confessions of I, Bonaparte.*
Basic beliefs: The Space Brothers are on their way. We would all benefit from a dose of past-life therapy.

Somewhere in the hills near Cajun in South California there used to be a huge sign bearing the legend 'Welcome Space Brothers 2001'. This was the year in which extraterrestrial beings called the Pleiadeans were supposed to land a fleet of 33 jewelled spaceships next to this sign on land that the Unarius Academy had bought specifically for the purpose. These kindly aliens were due to initiate nothing less than a spiritual renaissance for humankind, ending all war, poverty and plagues. Then the missionaries (there were going to be 30,000 on each ship) would invite Earth to become the 33rd and final member of the Interplanetary Confederation of Planets.

Unfortunately for all of us – and especially for the Unarius Academy, who have suffered a number of crushing blows in the last fifteen years or so – the Pleiadeans didn't arrive on schedule. The welcome sign, it transpired, was useless.

The vaguely rectal-sounding word Unarius is actually an acronym for Universal Articulate Interdimensional Understanding of Science. This educational organisation (the Unariuns, as they like to be known, vehemently deny that they're a religion as they have nothing in common with any other world religious beliefs and claim that their theories are based on 'science') was set up on Valentine's Day 1954 when founders Ernest and Ruth Norman first met.

Ernest and Ruth evolved a complex and (to outsiders) rambling belief system involving life on other worlds, life in other dimensions, angels, supernatural powers, intergalactic travel in massive flying saucers, channelling and reincarnation. There's also an evil space race in the mix too. They control the Orion Empire, which was responsible for the computer problems relating to the year 2000 and

all those funny stories over the years about alien abduction. Apparently, these were actually really just past-life memories of torture and brainwashing suffered at the hands of the Orions.

Ernest Norman claimed to have been both Jesus of Nazareth (he supposedly had the crucifixion scars to prove it) and the Egyptian god Osiris. Ruth Norman, meanwhile, said she'd lived 55 lives on Earth, among them were Socrates, Confucius, King Arthur, King Poseid of Atlantis and the Buddha. When Ernest Norman was causing trouble in Galilee as Jesus, she was his consort Mary Magdalene.

During their incarnation as the founders of Unarius, the couple explained that Earth is a kind of prison to which beings who have done terrible things in past lives return and where they have a chance at redemption. After Ernest passed away in the early 1970s (to take up a position on Mars, where he acts as Moderator of the Universe for the Interplanetary Confederation of Planets), Ruth brought past-life therapy to the forefront of Unariun activity. Films were made of members dressed in 'historical' outfits acting out the most significant scenes from their previous incarnations. The process was said to help them to resolve all the conflicts they didn't work out in their prior existences and to free them from residual negative energies. The inadvertently hilarious films were also shown on public access TV in America, together with talks from the sprightly seventy-something Ruth (she was born in 1900) dressed in kitsch pantomime-dame dresses, wearing sparkling tiaras and often wielding a wand. Her charismatic showmanship helped the society reach a peak of around 10,000 members in the 1980s and her prolific output of books (she wrote more than 80) helped top up the coffers.

Disaster struck in 1993, however, when Ruth died and therefore failed to live up to one of her most important promises: that she would be around to greet the Space Brothers when they arrived in 2001. Luckily, Ruth had a worthy successor for the leadership in the form of Charles Spiegel. Using the experience he had gained in past lives as Napoleon, Pontius Pilate and Satan (all detailed in his 536-page autobiography *The Confessions of I, Bonaparte*), Spiegel was able to steer his fellow Unariuns through the crisis of confidence.

Then the society took another hard knock in 1997, when 39 members of the Heaven's Gate cult committed suicide in Santa Fe, believing that they had been called to a spaceship behind the comet Hale-Bopp. The media descended on Unarius because of the apparent similarities in the two groups' belief systems, and Spiegel had to fight to convince concerned authorities that there was no room for suicide in the upbeat Unarius philosophy. He did have some good news for the reporters, though: one of the aliens he used to channel had told him that the luckless members of Heaven's Gate were currently in a healing ward on another planet.

Outsiders then gleefully predicted that Unarius would fall apart when 2001 arrived and the spaceships didn't – especially since Spiegel had by then also passed away, leaving control of the group to a committee. They hadn't reckoned on the cheerful resilience of the remaining Unariuns, however. This optimism was only bolstered when the Muons from the planet Myton used a member to channel the message that the fleet was still going to arrive – but no new date had yet been set. Even now, according to Unarius officials, a Pleiadean spacecraft is in the Earth's orbit, hovering invisibly. At the right time, it will land on a rising portion of Atlantis in the region of the Bermuda Triangle, carrying a thousand scientists from Myton. Another 32 flying saucers will then arrive and park on top of the first one to form a gigantic interplanetary learning centre – and to issue in a new Golden Age. It's going to be great.

The Unification Church, AKA The Moonies.
Founded: 1954.
Country of origin: Korea.
Gods and guiding voices: 'God', Jesus, Myung Moon.
Membership: 3 million.
Texts: Reverend Myung Moon: *Divine Principle.*
Basic beliefs: Jesus failed in his mission but Reverend Sun Myung Moon will fulfil it as God's designated Messiah. Liberals are bad. Right-wingers are good.

The members of the Unification Church are better known by their nickname, the Moonies. They're so called because of their leader, the Reverend Sun Myung Moon, an octogenarian who once appeared in the *Guinness Book of Records* for marrying the most couples in one go.

This prodigious feat was achieved in 1992 when Rev. Moon oversaw the wedding of 30,000 smiling followers at the Olympic Stadium in Seoul. He's conducted dozens of other mass weddings and, on current form, it's odds-on that he will become the most prolific tier of nuptial knots in recorded history.

Moon's interest in marriage is central to his philosophy. Marriage is an essential part of Unification Church morality and Moon claims that it's part of his work as a Messiah to splice as many couples (whose matches he has arranged) as possible. Meanwhile, he and his current wife (his third or fourth, depending on who you believe) provide the example of the perfect first family.

Moon teaches that his union and its progeny are, in fact, the fulfilment of God's plan for the world in the Garden of Eden. That scheme was all messed up in the first place when Eve dodged off and let the serpent have his way with her. Jesus was 'plan B', but he too failed to complete his mission. He was supposed to start the ideal race with Mary Magdelene, but was forestalled by all that awkward business relating to the cross. The worst thing about this for poor old Jesus was that, according to Moon, 'singles' cannot enter heaven. Luckily, Moon claims to have married the luckless son of God to a female in the spirit world so that he could gain entrance.

The reason that Moon marries so many couples together at once is simply that he's a very busy man. Small surprise there, since he's supposed to be the Second Coming. Meanwhile, the couples are

Words of Wisdom

❛ I will conquer and subjugate the world. I am your brain. ❜

Rev. Moon

probably pretty keen to enter married life because, although Moonies live ostensibly normal lives within the organisation, drinking, smoking and, crucially, premarital sex are strictly forbidden.

The huge weddings also have the potential to be a nice little earner. Each couple pays around $70 a head; a pretty significant amount when multiplied by 30,000. The Church needs the money. Its eventual aim is said to be to control the world under Moon – and that's going to take a lot of cash. Since it was founded in 1954, the organisation has been busily – and generally successfully – raising the necessary funds. One of the major accusations launched at the Moonies is that they are allowed to lie to the public in order to raise money. Certainly, followers have been caught selling flowers and gifts claiming that the proceeds would go to charity rather than helping to achieve world dominion for their leader. The Unification Church also has a baffling array of different affiliated organisations used to raise funds. It's been said that there are more than fifty in Britain alone, operating under such seemingly innocuous and unrelated names as the Kensington Garden Arts Society, the New World Singers and the International Conference on the Unity of the Sciences.

It's not just these fundraising eccentricities that have brought Moon's organisation under hostile fire in the past. After he started to expand out of Korea into Europe and America in the 1970s and early 1980s, the group became one of the major targets of the anti-cult movement. They were especially alarmed by the hair-raising allegations that ex-members were making about brainwashing and kidnapping within the Moonies. Then in 1982, Moon was convicted of conspiracy and filing false tax returns and made to serve thirteen months in Danbury Federal Penitentiary in the United States.

Since that time, Moon has done a lot of hard work to rehabilitate his image. Immediately after his release he launched a $5 million public relations campaign, began meeting members of the world's elite (especially leading US right-wingers) and started to buy up media titles like News World Communications. This corporation owns United Press International and the *Washington Times*, which has since run articles previously published by white-supremacist hate groups and quoted Nick Griffin, the head of Britain's fascist British National Party, as an authority on Muslim culture.

Moon has also received some hefty endorsements to support his cleaned-up credentials. He's claimed that no lesser figures than Jesus Christ, the Buddha and Muhammad have all professed themselves admirers. Recently, the Unification Church ran a two-page advert in the *Washington Times* asserting that 36 presidents from George Washington through to Richard Nixon gave their backing to Moon during a series of 'spirit world' conferences. Richard Nixon can be assumed to have been returning a favour. The avowedly right-wing Moon took out full-page adverts in major US newspapers defending 'President Richard M. Nixon' at the height of the Watergate controversy in the 1970s. When his message of 'Forgive, Love, Unite' was badly received, he then sent out missionaries to 120 countries to act in part as 'lightning rods' to receive some of the 'persecution'

Words of Wisdom

❛ In restoring man from evil sovereignty, we must cheat. ❜

Rev. Moon

directed at the jowly old crook. Perhaps more surprising, however, is Thomas Jefferson's willingness to add his name to the list of Moon's supporters. During his lifetime he was implacably opposed to the kind of theocratic government that Moon proposes. It must be presumed that a couple of hundred years of being dead has been enough to cause him to revise his opinions.

Moon hasn't just received help from dead ex-presidents. The elder George Bush has spoken at Moon-organised events while his son George W seems only too delighted to accept Moon's regular and large donations to Republican Party coffers (including $250,000 to help with Bush's inaugural bash in 2005). British prime ministers have been getting in on the act too. Ted Heath once made a lucrative appearance on the Moon platform.

All the same, Moon's behind-the-scenes success with his fellow right-wingers have failed to provide sufficient consolation for his continuing failure to convert the rest of society. He still rails against individualism – particularly all that 'free sex' in which men and women have the gall to choose partners without his sanction and approval. In a speech in December 2000 he even felt moved to advise: 'If a couple exists with that individualism, then the concave organ [meaning the vagina] should be sealed with concrete.'

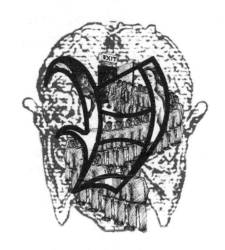

Vibrational Individuation Programme
Founded: Not known.
Country of origin: Australia.
Membership: 450.
Basic beliefs: Got to get those good vibrations happening ... and eat some offal.

The Vibrational Individuation Programme (VIP) claims to be a complementary health programme that uses nutrition to restore the body back to health. They say this is based on spiritual principles and supported by sound scientific knowledge and research.

According to Senator Grant Chapman, a politician who denounced the group to the Australian Federal Parliament, the leaders of the

Vibrational Individuation Programme also claim to be able to perform tests through people's wrists and surrounding muscles that can determine what food they should eat. Meanwhile, the diets they've prescribed have included drinking 756 glasses of water a day and eating brains and tongue 30 times a day. In fact, he said, these diets 'almost invariably' involve some form of offal.

These seemingly odd requirements are necessary to help balance the dieters' 'vibrations', Joan Philips, a director of the group, told an Australian newspaper in response to Chapman's allegations. She also strongly denied the senator's claims that VIP were targeting vulnerable pregnant women and controlling families. Ms Phillips did admit, however, that outsiders may regard her nutritional recommendations as 'odd' – but she said that all Australians should take her advice.

The Vibrational Individuation Programme also recommended that people wear only pink or white underwear.

Voluntary Human Extinction Movement

Founded: 1991.
Country of origin: USA.
Gods and guiding voices: Not applicable – this is a rational movement rather than a religion.
Membership: Around 250.
Basic beliefs: There are too many humans and they are a scourge on the planet Earth and its delicate ecology.

At first glance, the Voluntary Human Extinction Movement seems gloomy and self-defeating. After all, its most treasured aim is the eventual disappearance of the human race. However, while philanthropy probably isn't the right word for it, there is at least an admirable form of altruism at work behind their philosophy. They believe that humans should vacate the planet for the good of every other species. They say that we won't be missed as we aren't a part of any other creature's food chain, but our continuing presence is causing alarming rates of extinction and toxic degradation. In short, Earth would be better off without us.

The Movement – known as VHMENT for short (pronounced *vehement*, which is what the members claim they are) – is the brainchild of Les U Knight (say it quickly – Les added the 'U' to his name himself). It's the only child he'll ever have because he's taken the decision never to reproduce. They don't want war, starvation or mass murder. They just want us all to stop making more of us. 'Thank you,' they say, 'for not breeding.' Their motto is: 'May You Live Long and Die Out.'

Knight describes this nonviolent and gradual decline in the species as the humanitarian alternative to the problems that humans cause. It's a belief that he's held since the 1970s, but it wasn't until the early 1990s that he started widely publicising it and asking for volunteers with the regular publication of his newsletter *EXIT Times*. Unusually, issue number three of *EXIT Times* wasn't actually printed – in order to save paper. The Internet has solved this moral quandary, however, and Knight now explains his philosophy online at 'VHMENT.org'. Over the years, his ideas have reached millions of people (especially thanks to features in *Reader's Digest* magazine and on the Fox News Network), although researchers have suggested that so far there aren't many more than 230 subscribers to Knight's mailing list.

Knight himself is happy to admit that human extinction is a long-range goal. He says that even though there's virtually no chance of everybody in the world volunteering to stop breeding, the decision to do so is still morally correct. Be that as it may, most people would still regard his ideas as a little extreme. It's hard to see too many people joining VHMENT. Or, if too many people do join, it's hard to see it lasting long.

The Westboro Baptist Church

Founded: 1967.
Country of origin: USA.
Gods and guiding voices: 'God'.
Membership: Figures not available – although some estimates have been as low as 50.
Texts: The Bible.
Basic beliefs: God hates homosexuals. And Swedish people. But He likes bigoted old rednecks.

The Westboro Baptist Church has blown away the New Age Christian smokescreen about the God of love and forgiveness. Its members have actually read the Bible and have come to the inescapable conclusion that the God portrayed in the Old and New Testament is just as hate-filled, intolerant and homophobic as they are themselves. And that's pretty damn homophobic. In fact, the numerous anti-gay rants in the Bible have led them to declare that 'God hates fags' and so inspired their infamous, hate-filled website 'godhatesfags.com'. There they declare that all homosexuals will – and deserve to – burn in hell, and advocate the death penalty to hurry them on their way. All this, in spite of their own near pornographic fascination with the various gay sex acts that they describe on the site in salacious detail.

The Westboro Baptist Church was founded by Fred Phelps in 1967. Few people outside its base in Topeka, Kansas, the heart of Middle America, had heard of it until 1998. Then Phelps and several members of his clan (most of his congregation is made up of members of his family – he has thirteen children and more than fifty grandchildren) gained national notoriety in the US when they protested outside the funeral of Matthew Shepard, a gay college student who was beaten to a pulp in a homophobic attack. Since then they've left their compound in Topeka to travel up and down the country on protests. Carrying signs inscribed with messages like 'Turn or Burn', 'AIDS Cures Fags', as well as the ubiquitous 'God Hates Fags', they harass openly gay film stars, gay-rights activists and numerous dead people. The 'godhatesfags' website even contains pictures of members of Westboro Baptist Church dancing on the grave of pro-gay journalist Henry Clay Gold.

Homosexuals aren't the only ones unfortunate enough to fall victim

to Phelps's bile and bigotry. In the past he's attacked US presidential candidate John Kerry for being Jewish. Most bizarrely, he's also had a sustained dig at the Swedish nation. Phelps was incensed when a Swedish pastor, Åke Green, was sentenced to one month's imprisonment under hate-crimes legislation in his native country for regaling his congregation with a few of the more homophobic passages in the Bible. In response Phelps launched the website 'godhatessweden.com' and said that the Scandinavian nation was 'perverted', 'cursed' and 'damned'. When 20,000 Swedes were tragically declared missing after the 2005 Southeast Asian tsunami, Phelps saw it as cause for rejoicing. It was, he declared, God's judgement against the 'filthy faggot' Swedes and he said he hoped and prayed that the 20,000 were all dead. Even Pastor Green said he was deeply distressed by Phelps's actions, which he described as 'appalling'. Nevertheless, Phelps says that he intends to erect a monument to Pastor Green bearing the chilling legend 'Sweden Is Doomed'. Lovers of Volvos, pickled herrings and common decency the world over must hope that he is wrong.

Stop Press

Phelps and his organisation have recently published an article thanking God for the bombing of the London Underground 'wherein dozens were killed and hundreds seriously injured' and saying: 'Wish it were many more.' His website then went on to describe the UK as the 'Island of the Sodomite Damned' and Cherie Blair as a 'bitch barrister'. Charming.

XXXX

Founded: 1901.
Country of origin: Ireland.
Gods and guiding voices: 'God'.
Membership: Estimates vary between 10,000 and 160,000.
Texts: The Bible (though only the King James version is recognised.)
Basic beliefs: A unique and secretive form of Christianity based on the belief that the gospel can only be taught face to face.

As well as providing a handy way to crowbar the letter 'X' into this anthology, this organisation, which has consistently refused to give itself a name, is also fascinating in its own right.

It was the group's original founder William Irvine who insisted that they took no name. His policy has backfired dramatically. Because no one knows what to call them, everyone seems to give them a nickname. At various times and in various places the XXXX group have been called: The No Names, The No Secters, The Secret Sect, The Nameless House Sect, The Nameless House Church, The Church Without A Name, Die Namenlosen, Les Anonymes, The Way, The Jesus Way, The Pilgrims, The Black Stockings, The Tramps, The Tramp Preachers, The Go-Preachers, The Faith Missioners, The Dippers, The Workers, The Irvinites, The Cooneyites, The Carrollites, The Reidites, The Two-By-Twos, The Friends, The Saints, God's People, The New Testament Church, The Non-Denominational Church of England (or America, Australia, etc.), The Christian Church of

" THAT WAS RUBBISH, I THOUGHT
IT WAS GONNA BE LIKE THAT
CHILDREN OF GOD ONE WE
WENT TO "

England (or America, Australia, etc.), The Testimony of Jesus in England, The United Christian Conventions of Australia and New Zealand, The Christian Convention Church, The Truth and even The Damnation Army.

The exact theology of XXXX is difficult for outsiders to grasp. The group publishes few items. Their hymnbook, entitled *Hymns Old and New*, was published in 1951, and in 1987 a 'friends' list' giving names, addresses and phone numbers of members was made available. Since then there have been no official publications. Notes of sermons, taken from special meetings, are typed and passed among the friends, but all other note-taking is discouraged, because, as one senior member once explained, there are people in the world who want to find out 'what we believe'.

What is known is that Irvine believed that all preachers should be homeless, unpaid, journeying ministers. He held rallies where he challenged men and women to take vows of celibacy, poverty, submission and self-denial, and to go out into the world spreading the gospel. Hundreds travelled the English-speaking world, spreading Irvine's word, generally in groups of two (hence one of the more enduring nicknames, The Two-by-Twos). Irvine maintained that eventually these preachers would be able to visit other planets. He also taught that only those who heard this gospel from him – or at least heard it from people who had themselves heard it from him – would be granted salvation. This should have given him an unassailable position at the top of the group, but in 1914 he was excommunicated by his co-believers. His successor, Edward Cooney, was also thrown out in 1928. Strangely, the remaining members then agreed to never again admit that Irvine was their founder and many began to maintain that their nameless organisation had existed from the beginning of eternity. In the 1920s they also took on the mantle of secrecy and mystery that surrounds them to this day.

The group claims to have no rules or regulations, but there are a number of unspoken taboos, including swearing, dancing, going to the cinema, gambling, watching TV, reading Christian literature, and wearing jewellery. While they disposed of their original leaders, many of their early teachings have remained in place. Most notably, the strict dress codes laid down at the beginning of the twentieth century still apply, a matter of no small inconvenience to members, who generally have to maintain Victorian standards of clothing with shirts for men and long dresses or skirts for women. Additionally, ladies' long hair is usually worn in a bun and beards are frowned upon. Failure to conform can result in the slack dresser being thrown out of the group.

Little else can be said about the group with any certainty, other than that they're convinced that all outsiders are going to hell.

Yahweh Ben Yahweh and the Nation of Yahweh

Founded: 1979.
Country of origin: USA.
Gods and guiding voices: 'God', Yahweh Ben Yahweh.
Peak membership: 10,000.
Current membership: 1,000.
Texts: The Bible.
Basic beliefs: Yahweh Ben Yahweh is the son of God. He will lead his people to the Promised Land. You'd better not get in his way.

At Yahweh Ben Yahweh's trial in 1992, US federal prosecutor Richard Scruggs offered a summary of the heavily bearded defendant's religious and cultural development since the 1930s. He had gone from being a poor kid in a dusty Oklahoma town, to an airman, to a Nation of Islam leader, to a Christian evangelist with his own radio show, to a self-declared prophet at the centre of the religion he founded, to saying that he was the son of God.

'It took you a while to work your way up, didn't it?' said Scruggs.

'Certain things were revealed to me with time,' replied Yahweh Ben Yahweh, with typical implacability.

Yahweh Ben Yahweh's journey to that courtroom is worth a book in itself. He originally had the far more down-to-earth name of Hulon Mitchell Jnr and, as the prosecutor noted, he dragged himself out of his depression-era childhood, via the US airforce, to become a leading preacher in the Nation of Islam. He left that organisation under something of a cloud, having been accused of fleecing church coffers to the tune of $50,000 and molesting young female members of his flock. Then, as well as becoming a radio gospel preacher, he had started to build what would eventually become a vast fortune by offering the services of his 'blessed prayer cloth', which helped the lame walk and others to get their hands on that Cadillac or new house that they needed. 'God wants you to be rich!' declared Mitchell Jnr in an early intimation of the **Rev Creflo Dollar**.

In spite of its financial success, the church he built up fell apart in the mid-1970s when the congregation started squabbling over communal property and threatened to sue Mitchell for fraud. It was then that he finally realised that he was the son of God – and a god himself. He ditched the inconvenient Mitchell Jnr appellation, took on the more resonant and relevant title of Yahweh Ben Yahweh (it's Hebrew for 'God, son of God') and moved to Miami.

In the sunny Florida capital, Yahweh Ben Yahweh preached an extreme militant creed. He labelled Caucasians as 'white devils' and said that the 'so-called black people in America' were in reality the descendants of Abraham, Isaac, and Jacob – the true 'chosen people' of Yahweh, the God of the Bible (who also happened to be Yahweh Ben Yahweh's father). He said that he was going to lead his fellow 'true Jews' from oppression, and attracted thousands of followers. The donations he persuaded them to hand over were used to help set up a small business empire in Miami. As well as their huge headquarters, 'The Temple of Love', the Yahwehs owned a four-storey apartment building, hotels by the ocean, restaurants, retail stores, supermarkets and houses as well as hundreds of vans, buses and lorries, which were all painted crisp white, to match the distinctive white robes and turbans worn by Yahweh Ben Yahweh and his followers.

In spite of this success, the divine prophet had been growing increasingly paranoid about the things other members of the Nation of Yahweh were saying about him. Especially when some started putting about the rumour that – contrary to his vow of chastity – Yahweh Ben Yahweh was making night visits to the women's quarters in the aptly named Temple of Love. Shortly after some of these 'infidel' rumourmongers began to defect from the church, they died in mysterious and violent circumstances. Around that time Yahweh Ben Yahweh also formed a secret group for his own protection called the

Words of Wisdom

' Whoever does not want me to rule over them, those are my enemies. And if you are my enemy, you must die. (You) must be killed … I want to see it … I want to see your head come off personally. I want to see the blood seep from your vein, you know that jugular vein. I want to see it … you won't be able to see it seep, but you'll feel that sword when it bites your neck. I can't wait to see that. What a pleasure! '

Yahweh Ben Yahweh

Words of Wisdom

' When we take the next head, we're going to put the head in a basket on a post so the whole city can see it and fear Yahweh. '

Yahweh Ben Yahweh

Brotherhood. They proved their loyalty to their leader by taking on missions as 'Death Angels' and going out to kill randomly chosen 'white devils'.

Despite the murders, the Yahwehs continued to prosper. By 1990 their assets were estimated at $100 million (they even claimed the figure was closer to $250 million). Yahweh Ben Yahweh himself was so well regarded in his chosen city that Miami's Mayor Xavier Suarez declared 7 October 1990 'Yahweh Ben Yahweh Day'.

Even then, however, the noose was tightening around the organisation. The chief enforcer of the Brotherhood, Robert Rozier, a former professional American-football player, had been arrested for his part in a 1986 murder. At first he answered all questions with the words 'Praise Yahweh!' but as he began to realise how much jail time he faced he agreed to plea-bargain and turned witness against the organisation. A few weeks after Mayor Suarez's announcement of Yahweh Ben Yahweh Day, Yahweh himself was arrested in New Orleans. 'Obviously I was wrong,' Suarez said when reporters harangued him about his calendar arrangements. Apparently, he was quite 'testy' about the whole thing.

By the time Yahweh Ben Yahweh came to trial in 1992, fourteen corpses had been traced back to the Temple of Love. Some had been decapitated with machetes, some had had their ears cut off. The presiding judge called it the most violent case ever to come before a federal court. The authorities were so scared of reprisals that they surrounded the building where the trial took place with SWAT teams.

On the stand, Yahweh Ben Yahweh described himself as the 'grand master of the celestial lodge, the architect of the universe'. He coolly denied everything and said that his religion was about love. The prosecution was unable to connect him directly to any of the murders, but he served nine years for 'conspiracy'. In August 2001, he walked out a free man. The Yahwehs have been recruiting ever since.

A Silly Old Cult!
Sabbatai Zevi
Alive: 1626–76.
Country of origin: Turkey.
Membership: Uncounted millions.
Texts: The Torah.
Basic beliefs: Sabbatai Zevi is the Messiah and it doesn't matter if he denies it because he doesn't mean it.

Unlike most of the self-proclaimed Messiahs that stalk through these pages, Sabbatai Zevi managed to survive long enough to die of natural causes. What's more, he got there without killing anybody else.

Zevi's longevity can largely be attributed to his sharp intelligence.

Even as a child his knowledge of Jewish scriptures and his kabbalistic wisdom was so impressive that his father regarded him as some kind of deity. He himself didn't agree, until the age of 22 when he heard about the massacre of Poland's Jews at the hands of the Cossacks. He became convinced that he *was* the Messiah and determined to lead his people away from these horrors and into the Holy Land.

That realisation came in 1648. Using his knowledge of the Torah, Zevi worked out that he wouldn't have to lead his followers away until the supposedly apocalyptic year 1666. Until then, he bided his time, gathering supporters and spreading his message. Occasionally he would perform what his contemporaries described as 'strange acts' to keep people interested.

For instance, in his home town of Smyrna, Zevi walked into a Jewish temple and cried out the name of God in Hebrew. Jews, like Christians, then thought that this name, the Tetragrammaton 'YHWH' was too holy to speak. In fact, the only person who was permitted to say it aloud was the High Priest in Jerusalem (and then only on the annual Day of Atonement). This 'strange act' was shocking enough to ensure that he was thrown straight out of town. On a later occasion, he walked around the Turkish town of Salonica (now Thessaloniki in Greece) carrying a basket of fish, proclaiming it was the age of Pisces and that soon all Jews would be released from their bondage. His career in Salonica came to an end when he invited friends to a feast, where he took a scroll of the Old Testament Book of Law into his arms as if it were a woman and took it to a marriage canopy he had set up.

This symbolic wedding of the Messiah and the Law outraged the local rabbis so much that they had him exiled – again.

As Zevi had planned, the bizarre nuptials greatly increased his fame. He moved on to Jerusalem where he used to sing psalms all night long in his melodious voice – or occasionally even the odd bawdy Spanish love song – and gathered ever larger numbers around him like the Pied Piper. In Jerusalem he also met Nathan Ashkenazi, a prolific writer who began to trumpet Zevi's deeds and forthcoming ascension in graphic epistles (full of seven-headed snakes and Zevi blasting his enemies with fire erupting from his mouth), which he sent around the world.

Meanwhile, Zevi did his part through fulfilling an Old Testament prophecy by marrying a prostitute. This was the famously unchaste Sarah, by all accounts pretty hot stuff, and ideal for Zevi as she'd been convinced since childhood that she would marry the Messiah. Unfortunately, the marriage eventually ended in divorce because it was never consummated. Zevi maintained his reputation, however, by carrying out even more 'strange acts'. They became increasingly aggressive and shocking as 1666 drew nearer. In December 1665, for example, he burst into a synagogue during Sabbath prayers, and harangued and bullied the worshippers until they, too, all pronounced the name of 'Yahweh' with him.

By then, he was powerful enough to get away with it. His supporters were everywhere. Many were in a frenzy of religious ecstasy. They could be spotted all over Europe and the Near East, rolling naked in snow, whipping themselves, starving themselves and even digging themselves into the ground so that only their heads stuck out. From Germany to Yemen the faithful were selling all their properties in preparation to travel to meet their Messiah in Jerusalem. In London, Samuel Pepys recorded in his diary that local gamblers were offering ten-to-one odds that 'a certain person' would 'within these two years' be recognised 'by all the princes of the East … as the King of the world, in the same manner we do the King of England, and that this man is the true Messiah.' It's been estimated that up to a third of the Jewish world believed Zevi to be the Messiah.

Early in 1666, Zevi decided it was time to act. He chartered a ship to Constantinople where he intended to fulfil a prophecy by lifting the crown from the head of the Sultan of the Ottoman Empire. But things didn't go according to plan. As the ship docked the Sultan's ambassador did indeed come to greet Zevi but promptly boxed his ears. He was then thrown into jail.

In spite of these setbacks, Zevi was smart enough to ensure that enough palms were greased to enable him to reside there in some style. It was his next move that showed his true intelligence, however. After a few months, the Sultan summoned Zevi and told him that he must either convert to Islam or die. A contemporary rabbi described the would-be Messiah's decision: 'He began grovelling on the ground before the Sultan, begging that he might be allowed to take refuge in the Sultan's religion … He insulted the Jewish faith and profaned God's name, in full public view.'

The Sultan was so delighted that he gave Zevi a well-paid sinecure as a doorkeeper.

Zevi was able to keep most of his disappointed followers happy by telling them he hadn't converted at all. Meanwhile, he managed to please the Sultan by converting some of his own Jewish followers to Islam – and ensured his followers stayed onside by converting a few local Muslims to his unique form of Judaism. The resulting hybrid sect – the Donehs – still survives to this day (at the last count there were reckoned to be around 15,000 in Iran and Turkey); a continuing testament to the persuasive powers of Sabbatai Zevi. He himself died of natural causes in Albania, openly admitting that he was a charlatan and still the subject of devotion for thousands of adoring followers.

Glossary

Ascetic

A monk or hermit, or pertaining to the exercise of extremely rigorous self-discipline. The term became popular in the Western world in the first few centuries AD when early Christians like St Antony would dash off into the desert, starve themselves half to death, belabour themselves with birch-wood and come back raving about hallucinatory fights with Satan. Some modern Christian monks could be said to follow aspects of the ascetic lifestyle, but if you want to check out a bona fide hard-core practitioner nowadays, your best bet is to head to India or Nepal and find a Sadhu. There, these worshippers of the Hindu god Siva have epitomised the ascetic ideal since the time of Alexander the Great, living chaste lives and often achieving unbelievable feats of endurance and privation: sitting in the same place, immobile for twenty years, keeping one arm raised for so long it atrophies, walking on shoes lined with nails or tying their own bodies into yogic knots.

Usage:

'He doesn't drink, smoke or laugh. He lives a very ascetic lifestyle.'

Or

'Melania the Younger was an ascetic. She spent most of her time nailed inside a box that was too small for her limbs and only ate on Tuesdays.'

Ashram

A word from India meaning a place of religious retreat, sanctuary or hermitage.

Usage:

'The better-looking boys came to dread their daily visits to the ashram.'

Book of Revelation

The last book of the New Testament, which contains an awful lot of bad news for the long-term future of mankind. Supposedly written by St John, its prophecies of eyes of fire, seas of blood, scarlet beasts and the number of the beast (666) have inspired countless works of art, prog-rock anthems and, of course, extreme religious groups. The bit about 'malignant sores' is particularly bracing reading. The book also claims that Jesus Christ is coming 'quickly', which has been a source of great confusion among true believers for almost 2,000 years.

(see also 'The Seven Seals')

Usages:

'You will be scorched with fire, covered in sores, gnaw your tongue from pain, watch the sea turn to blood, reap the Grapes of Wrath, see your crops devoured by locusts, watch the stars fall to Earth, be killed by the sword, hunger and the beasts of the earth. Just like it says in the Book of Revelation, sinner.'

Or

'We'll always be league champions!'
'That's not what it says in the Book of Revelation.'

Brainwashing

The forcible implantation of new ideas in the mind of a person and the elimination of established ones. The term first became popular during the Korean War when American POWs captured by the North Koreans came back garbling about how great they thought Communism was. Whether brainwashing really exists – and whether it's possible to coerce an unwilling subject into taking on a new belief – has been a matter of great debate ever since. Some maintain that all religions, with their use of ritual, chanting and liturgy, practise forms of brainwashing. Others say that people can only take on beliefs of their own freewill.

Usage:

'I believe it because it's absurd.'

'No, you believe it because you've been brainwashed from an early age.'

The Day of Atonement

Specifically, this is Yom Kippur, the most solemn day in the Jewish calendar, a day of fasting and penitence. More loosely, however, it is used to describe the time when the events described in the book of Revelation kick off.

Usages:

'You may be laughing now, but you'll be weeping blood on the Day of Atonement.'

David

David in the Old Testament slew Goliath and went on to be King of the Hebrews. Several Old Testament prophecies state that the Messiah will come from 'David's line' and some suggest that he too will be called David. Hence the interest from cult leaders like the Children Of God's David Berg and the Branch Davidian's David Koresh.

Deprogrammer

Deprogrammers are people who are employed (generally by parents or concerned friends and relatives) to extract people from cults. They are generally firmly opposed to cult activity. They see cult members as 'victims' and aim to take them away from their current situation so that they can be made to understand that they have been (supposedly) taught a pack of lies and that they're the victims of psychological abuse. In the 1980s, some deprogrammers gained almost as bad a reputation as the cults themselves, thanks to the tactics they used to capture members' attention, which included kidnapping and forced restraint. On the other hand, there are also hundreds of people who are extremely grateful to deprogrammers – and considerably better off because of them.

Usage:

'The deprogrammer helped me to realise that I wouldn't necessarily be condemned to eternal damnation just for having my hair cut.'

Or

'I'm going to sue that bastard deprogrammer for tying my hands with duct tape and throwing me into the boot of his car.'

Disfellowshipping

When Jehovah's Witnesses break their society's strict moral code they are shunned and ostracised from their community. This process is known as disfellowshipping. It is possible for individuals to be taken back into the fold if they can prove that they sincerely repent of their 'misdeeds'. However, it must be presumed that this is an uphill struggle for the penitent, as everyone else has been told to ignore them.

The End, End Times

The End with a capital 'E' generally refers to the hectic events described in the book of Revelation. Although any other doom-laden prophecies are equally applicable.

Usages:

'The End is nigh!'

Guru

Originally a term describing a Hindu spiritual teacher or head of a religious sect, guru has more recently come to refer to just about anyone with a strong opinion and influence on subjects as diverse as economics, health foods and love-making.

Usages:

'Teach us, Guru, about the divinity of all things.'

Or

'Well, I was just starting the menopause when I sought out my guru in his ashram.'

Or

'I don't know if I should eat that. It might taste too good. I'll have to ask my guru.'

Jehovah

Interestingly, the word Jehovah comes from an eighteenth-century English mistranslation of the Hebrew tetragrammatton, YHWH, the personal name for the Hebrew God. For many years scholars have preferred the transliteration Yahweh – but since the word Jehovah has been a central plank of their belief system for so long, the Jehovah's Witnesses are pretty stuck with it – even though in every other respect they claim that their version of the Bible, The New World Translation, is the plainest and most literal.

Jesus Christ

According to the New Testament, Jesus is the son of God, Messiah, and the Way and the Light. According to the Koran, he was a major prophet. According to humanists, he was just some bloke with big ideas.

Usages:

'In the name of Jesus Christ Our Lord, Amen'

Or

'I over did it last night! Ooh my head hurts! Oh dear! Christ on a bike!'

Kabbalah (also cabbala, qabalah, or various other spellings)

The name given in post-biblical Hebrew to the oral tradition handed down from Moses to the rabbis. From the thirteenth century onwards it has also been applied to a tradition of the mystical interpretation of the Old Testament. It is this tradition from which the Kabbalah Centre derives its name.

Usages:

'He handed down the secrets of the kabbalah.'

Or

'That Kabbalah water is surprisingly expensive.'

The Koran

The holy book of Islam composed of the revelations that came to the prophet Muhammad.

Usages:

'Cat Stevens read the Koran and soon after declared his faith in Islam.'

Lingam

A representation of a penis, generally made out of stone and most often associated with the Hindu god Siva.

Usage:

'The guru amazed the crowd by coughing up a small, perfectly formed lingam.'

Martin Luther

The man who kick-started the reformation by arguing that salvation is granted because of faith, not deeds. He suffered from chronic constipation and claimed that he was actually sitting on the throne when he was inspired to launch his attacks on papal abuses.

Messiah

The expected ruler and deliverer of the Jewish people whose coming is prophesied in the Old Testament. Christians believe that Jesus is the Messiah, but many other figures in history (such as Joachim of Fiore, Sabbatai Zevi and David Koresh of the Branch Davidians) have also claimed this title.

Usage:

'Messiah! Lord! Teach us!'

Or

'He's not the Messiah, he's a very naughty boy.'

Proselytising

The attempt to convert a person from one opinion or belief to another.

Qabalah (see kabbalah)

The Rapture

Some Christian groups believe in an End Time scenario in which all true believers are taken from the Earth in 'the twinkling of an eye' while nonbelievers are left behind to endure the fire and blood of the tribulation (as described in the book of Revelation). The moment at which the believers are whisked off to heaven is known as the 'Rapture'. It's particularly based on two passages from the Bible. The first is 1 Corinthians 15:51–52 where Paul promises: 'We shall not all sleep, but we shall all be changed, in a moment, in the twinkling of an eye, at the last trump: for the trumpet shall sound, and the dead shall be raised incorruptible, and we shall be changed.' The second is Thessalonians 4:17, which states that believers will 'be caught up together … in the clouds to meet the Lord Jesus Christ in the air'. Hence the interest of the Millerites in jumping into the air from tall buildings.

The term also describes religious ecstasy.

Usages:

'He jumped out of the tree believing that the Rapture was about to come and he'd be whisked off to heaven. Actually, he cracked open his skull.'

Sannyasins

In the Hindu religion, a Sannyasin is someone who has given up the material world to concentrate on the spiritual. His or her ultimate aim is to achieve enlightenment and liberation. It's obvious why Bhagwan

Shree Rajneesh gave this appellation to his followers, but many Orthodox Hindus do not accept that Rajneesh's people can be true Sannyasins and even find the use of the term in this context insulting.

Satan (also known as Old Nick, Old Scratch, Lucifer, The Devil, The Father of Lies, The Prince of Darkness, The Fallen Angel, Beelzebub, The Serpent)

The bad guy in the Christian Bible and the star of Milton's *Paradise Lost*. Said to be fond of prodding sinners with his pitchfork and laughing at funerals. Is also famous for teaching Robert Johnson to play the blues.

Usages:

'Get thee behind me, Satan!'

The Seven Seals

One of the episodes in the book of Revelation is the opening of the Seven Seals on a mysterious scroll held by 'The Lamb'. As each seal is opened it brings with it a variety of calamities for the Earth. The first four Seals bring about the arrival of a 'Conqueror' who, not surprisingly, 'goes out conquering and to conquer' and the three other Riders of the Apocalypse: War, Famine and Death in turn. The fifth Seal makes martyrs cry, the sixth Seal causes cosmic disturbances and the seventh causes seven trumpets to peal. These trumpet peals cause all green grass to 'burn up', turn a third of the seas to blood, cause a star to fall from heaven (which turns a third of all waters in the world to bitter wormwood), turn a third of the world to darkness, bring out plagues of locusts from the Bottomless Pit (to torment all men without the seal of God on their heads for five months), release four angels (who proceed to kill a third of all mankind) and proclaim the kingdom of God. It's a strange book.

(see also 'Book of Revelation')

The Talmud

The Talmud is a body of Jewish ceremonial law and legend purportedly written by rabbinical scholars in the fifth century BC, based on an oral tradition.

Ten Lost Tribes Of Israel

Ten tribes said to be from the Biblical Kingdom of Israel. According to some readings of the Old Testament, they were taken captive by Assyria in 721 BC. After that, they either merged with the Assyrians or dispersed around the globe. Whether they actually existed, or what happened to them, are the subjects of enough speculation and bizarre theory to fill libraries.

Tithe

A tax or levy of ten per cent from an individual's annual income.

Usage:

'We need the tithe to maintain the church buildings. The fact that I have a new Mercedes is entirely coincidental.'

The Torah

Torah means the law, or instruction. It is the written law of the Jewish faith (the Talmud is the oral law, which deals with the application of the Torah). The term refers specifically to the first five books of the Old Testament, the books relating to Moses, but can be used more generally to refer to any kind of biblical teachings or philosophy.

Xenu

A galactic ruler who brought billions of people to Earth 75 million years ago, stacked them around volcanoes, blew them up with hydrogen bombs and then forced their souls to watch nasty films. According to L Ron Hubbard, founder of the Church of Scientology.

Yahweh

The name for God that most closely translates the Hebrew Tetragrammaton 'YHWH' into English. This word was only supposed to have been pronounced by man when the priest in the Temple on the Mount in Jerusalem met the Messiah and issued in the end of the world. Anyone else who uttered it risked being struck by lightning. Recently, however, many cult leaders have taken the name as their own and seem to have escaped unscathed. So far …

Usage:

'Of course I'm right. I'm Yahweh.'

Zohar

A mystical commentary on the Torah made up from a group of books written in medieval Aramaic and Hebrew. Contains mystical discussions of the nature of God, sin and the structure of the universe. One of the most important works in the Kabbalah tradition.

Usage:

'Even though he couldn't read Hebrew, he shelled out a big sum of money for a copy of the Zohar. When he escaped the cult he sold it on eBay at a considerable loss.'

Appendix 1

BEYOND BELIEF

The hardline anti-homosexual Christian organisations in this book may be made up of hateful old bigots, but their biblical knowledge is sound. Here's a nasty selection of passages from the 'holy book' about the need to persecute men practising gay sex.

Leviticus 18:22
You shall not lie with a man as with a woman, it is an abomination.

Leviticus 20:13
If a man lies with a male as he lies with a woman, both of them have committed an abomination. They shall surely be put to death. Their blood shall be upon them.

Romans 1:26–32
For even their women exchanged the natural use of what is against nature. Likewise the men leaving the natural use of the women, burned in their lust for one another, men with men committing what is shameful and receiving in themselves the penalty of their error which was due ... Being filled with unrighteousness, sexual immorality, wickedness

… they are whisperers, backbiters, haters of God, violent, proud, boasters, inventors of evil things, disobedient to parents, undiscerning, untrustworthy, unloving, unforgiving, unmerciful; who knowing the righteous judgement of God that those who practise such things are worthy of death …

For the story of Sodom and Gomorrah meanwhile, look up Genesis, chapter 19. Apparently it's OK to offer up your daughters to be raped by marauding armies but not to know men 'carnally'.

Appendix 2

The Mountain Meadows Massacre

The Church of Jesus Christ of Latter-day Saints recognise their leaders as divinely inspired prophets and their teachings as sacred. Sometimes, this can be tricky to deal with politically. One of the less well-known Mormon policies is that of blood atonement. The prophet Brigham Young taught that certain sins could only be amended for with a man's own blood. Killing can be a righteous act. 'Loving our neighbours as ourselves ... if he wants salvation and it is necessary to spill his blood ... spill it,' he said. This policy found its most chilling fulfilment in the Mountain Meadows Massacre when Brigham Young ordered his co-religionists to attack a party of emigrants who were crossing Mormon land on the way to California in 1857. One hundred and twenty men, women and children were massacred.

Some modern adherents of the Church of Jesus Christ Of Latter-day Saints have denied that the policy ever existed. However, many still put forward the idea that certain 'grievous sins' place the sinner 'beyond the reach of Christ's atoning blood' as a justification for capital punishment.

Appendix 3

The Book of Mormon

While Joseph Smith slaved away behind his screen producing the Book of Mormon he was largely left in peace. At some point during the process, however, an acquaintance of the prophet, one Martin Harris, called round and Smith despatched him to New York carrying a piece of paper with some of the 'reformed Egyptian' hieroglyphs on it. Harris took the paper to a professor named Anton, who issued him a certificate saying they were genuine – but then ripped it up on discovering that the characters were supposed to have been sent by an angel. So, tragically, the only piece of impartial evidence for the existence of the plates – and reformed Egyptian – was destroyed. (Smith returned the original plates to Moroni as soon as he had finished the translation. The book does contain several testimonies of other people who claim to have seen the plates – but they were all church leaders, or the relatives of church leaders.)

The work Smith eventually produced, the Book Of Mormon, is the cornerstone of the Mormon faith. Among a lot of moralistic preaching, it explains that America had originally been settled by people from the Tower of Babel, but that these inhabitants had degenerated and perished as a result of their own immorality. A later group of Jews then ended up in South America after fleeing Babylonian captivity. They divided into warring factions, the Nephites and the Lamanites. After his death on the cross, Jesus Christ appeared among these peoples and preached again. But the factions continued fighting and the Lamanites nearly wiped out the Nephites (the price of their victory was a curse – dark skin). After the final defeat, the prophet of the Nephites, Mormon, wrote up the history on gold plates and buried them on the hill – where Smith was to find them more than a thousand years later.

Critics have found it strange that, although it was supposedly written many centuries before the 1611 King James Bible, many passages appear to have been lifted verbatim from that book, complete with its translation errors. They also point out anachronisms like references to the ancient Hebrew use of steel and to domestic animals that weren't around at the time. Similarly, the book describes American Indians using weapons for which there is no archaeological evidence. Oddest of all, Mormon described elephants roaming around in places where there is no evidence elephants ever roamed.

Other investigators have found an earlier novel by the Reverend Simon Spalding that bears a marked similarity to much of the Book Of Mormon. There's also another book, *The View Of The Hebrews,* by the Rev. Ethan Smith (written in 1824, three years before Joseph Smith started work), which also contains many passages echoed in the Latter-day Saints' holy book.

Appendix 4

Catholic Guilt

The claim that the Catholic Church has caused more deaths than any other organisation in history is quite strong. So here's some backup.

325: In accepting the direction of Constantine at the Council of Nicaea, the Catholic Church began a long tradition of cosying up to absolute rulers and providing them moral legitimacy. The theory of the divine rights of kings helped to ensure that unaccountable despots would control Europe until the eighteenth century.

371–2: The first witch-hunts were instituted by the Roman Emperor Valens at the church's behest. The historian Ammianus described 'a throng of men of almost all ranks who it would be difficult to enumerate by name' meeting the sword.

385: Priscillian of Avila became the first man to be executed for heresy. Over the centuries, uncounted thousands would join him.

404: St Augustine (still one of the most revered and influential figures in the Catholic Church) started a long unhealthy tradition by recommending that his rivals in North Africa, the Donatists, be beaten with rods and tortured.

1050: Building work began on Cluny Cathedral. An estimated 100,000 people died during its construction – and they were on the

Church's side! The huge edifice is now a ruin, destroyed during World War II.

1095: Pope Urban II called for a large invasion force to take Jerusalem from the Muslims. The First Crusade began. In the fury that followed mobs massacred Jews throughout Europe, Orthodox Christians in the East were attacked and Christian knights rampaged throughout the Middle East. In 1099 the Crusaders took Jerusalem and massacred the Muslim population.

1202: The ironically named Pope Innocent III instituted the Fourth Crusade. Bizarrely, this ended with the sack of the Byzantine Christian city of Constantinople.

1209: In a long-running war against members of the Cathar heresy in France, the town of Béziers was captured and the population slaughtered by Catholic forces headed by the Papal legate, the Abbot of Citeaux. When he was asked how to distinguish between the Catholics and Cathars, witnesses said that the Abbot replied: 'Kill them all, God will know his own.'

1483: Tomas de Torquemada was appointed as the head of the Spanish Inquisition. Between 4,000 and 8,000 Jews were burned alive during the next fifteen years. A smaller, but significant, number of Moors also met their deaths. A further 125,000 were tried (and almost certainly tortured) in Church tribunals as suspected heretics. The Spanish Inquisition continued to function – with varying degrees of savagery – until 1834. There were also several other Inquisitions throughout Europe and the New World.

1484: Pope Innocent VIII issued a Papal Bull instigating a major wave of European witch-hunts. Over the next two centuries an estimated 500,000 were killed and unknown hundreds of thousands more were tortured.

1492: Columbus discovered America. Centuries of plunder and genocide followed. The colonialism was all endorsed and encouraged by the Catholic Church – and the crimes often carried out by its representatives.

1521: The Edict of Worms forbade the teaching of Lutheranism throughout the Holy Roman Empire. Centuries of religious wars followed.

1559: First edition of the index of prohibited books published.

1600: Giordano Bruno was burned at the stake for positing the infinite size of the universe.

1633: Galileo was tortured and imprisoned for stating that the Earth is not the centre of the universe. He was forced to recant his theories at a show trial of the Inquisition of Rome.

1864: Pope Pius IX produced the Syllabus of Errors condemning freedom of religion and the separation of church and state.

1900s to 1960s: Aboriginal Australian children were forcibly removed from their families by Catholic missionaries to be brought up in white foster families or institutions (where they were often abused). Pope John Paul II later apologised.

1924: Pope Pius XI forbade the Italian Catholic Popular Party to work with the Socialist Party against the fascist leader Mussolini.

1930: Pope Pius XI persuaded the German Catholic Centre Party to reject co-operation with the Social Democratic Party against the Nazis. Then in 1933, he had the party agree to the Enabling Law, which gave Hitler dictatorial powers. He also signed a friendship treaty, called the Concordat, with the Nazi leader. Hitler said: 'The Concordat gave Germany an opportunity and created a sense of trust that was particularly significant in the developing struggle against international Jewry.'

1936: The Catholic priesthood in Spain supported Franco in his overthrow of a democratically elected government. They stood behind his fascist rule until 1975.

1948: The 32nd edition of the index of prohibited books was published. There were 4,000 titles featured on the list, including works by Daniel Defoe, Copernicus and Jean-Paul Sartre. In 1966, the prohibitions were relaxed, although it remains a sin for Catholics to read books 'injurious' to their faith or morals.

1985: The Vatican declared that homosexuality is 'an intrinsic moral evil' and must be seen as 'an objective disorder'.

1990s to present: As AIDS ravaged Africa the Catholic Church maintained it was a mortal sin to use condoms. Several leading African Catholics were even caught telling their followers that condoms had little holes in them through which the HIV virus could penetrate and that they were therefore useless. Unknown millions have contracted the virus.

Further Reading

Far too many arcane, weird and wonderful books and news reports were used in researching this book to list here. The following is just a selection of the most helpful or otherwise interesting titles.

Aitch, Iain. *A Fete Worse Than Death*. London, Review, 2004

Bhaktivedanata, His Divine Grace AC. *The Bhagavad-Gita As It Is*. Borehamwood, Herts, The Bhaktivedanta Book Trust, 1986

Booth, Martin. *A Magick Life: A Biography of Aleister Crowley*. London, Coronet Books, 2000

Brown, Dan. *The Da Vinci Code*. London, Corgi, 2004

Caddy, Eileen. *The Spirit of Findhorn*. Findhorn, Forres, Findhorn Press, 1977

Crowley, Aleister. *Book IV*. New York, Red Wheel, 1987

Del Carmen Tapia, Maria. *Beyond the Threshold: A Life in Opus Dei*. New York, Continuum, 1997

Donaldson, William. *Brewer's Rogues, Villains and Eccentrics*. London, Cassell, 2002

Eide, Rita. *The Celestial Voice Of Diana*. Findhorn, Forres, Findhorn Press, 1999

Fraser, Antonia. *The Weaker Vessel*. London, Phoenix Press, 2002

Goldhill, Simon. *Love, Sex and Tragedy*. London, John Murray, 2004

Guest, Tim. *My Life in Orange*. London, Granta Books, 2004

Hammond, NGL and Scullard, HH. *The Oxford Classical Dictionary*.

Oxford, Oxford University Press, 1970

Harris, Marvin. *Cows, Pigs, Wars and Witches*. New York, Vintage Books, 1989

Heard, Alex. *Apocalypse Pretty Soon*. New York, Doubleday, 1999

Hubbard, L Ron. *Dianetics*. Redhill, Surrey, New Era Publications, 1986

Kossy, Donna. *Kooks*. Los Angeles, Feral House, 1994

LaVey, Anton. *The Satanic Bible*. New York, Avon Books, 1969

Larson, Bob. *Larson's New Book of Cults*. Wheaton, Illinois, Tyndale House Publishers, Inc., 1989

Shaw, William. *Spying In Guruland*. London, Fourth Estate, 1994

Smith, Joseph, Mormon and Moroni. The Book of Mormon. Salt Lake City, Utah, The Church of Jesus Christ of Latter Day Saints, 1981

Twain, Mark. *Roughing It*. London, Penguin Books, 1981

Wheen, Francis. *How Mumbo Jumbo Conquered The World*. London, Harper Perennial, 2004

Wilson, Colin and Damon. *World Famous Cults and Fanatics*. London, Magpie Books, 1992

Wallace, Danny. *Join Me*. London, Ebury Press, 2004

'Yahweh'. The Bible.

There are also countless websites out there made by and about cults and religious fanatics. The excellent archives at 'www.rickross.com' and 'wikipedia.org' are good starting points for anyone interested in further research.